CORKSCREWS
IN THE
KITCHEN

A GATEWAY TO WINE AND FOOD

by Arlene Taveroff

Illustrated by Lidia Wolchov

Cover Photos by Frank Prazak

Published by Kylix International Ltd.

Other publications from Kylix International Ltd.:

Wine Tidings magazine; eight issues per year, first published 1974.
Gateway to Wine, 1981; second printing 1983; revised 1985.
Gateway to Wine & Health, Herbert M. Baus, 1983.
Pocket Wine Record, 1982.

Canadian Cataloguing in Publication Data

Taveroff, Arlene, 1948-
  Gateway to wine and food

Includes Index.
ISBN 0-919571-08-5

1. Wine and wine making.   2.Cookery.
I. Title.

TP548.T39 1985   641.2'2   C85-090030-1

KYLIX INTERNATIONAL LTD.
Montreal, Canada 1985

FOREWORD

Most books tell only half the story! They deal with wine. Or they deal with food. A few go as far as devoting an entire chapter to food and wine, however few go into enough detail to really be helpful.

For example what do you do when a cookbook suggests that a certain recipe would go perfectly with Château Thisorthat and you've never heard of it, never mind stored it in your cellar? Or what if you are planning a dinner party and you want to feature that special bottle you have been saving? With what do you serve it? The chapters on Wine and Food never seem to mention *your* favourite wine.

See what I mean? It's frustrating, because most books are too narrow in their scope. They never really attack wine and food as a subject in itself. They ignore that all important interface.

That is the reason for this book. I want to bridge the gap between the world of wine and the world of food. After all, most of us drink wine with food more often than without it and like people, wines can change depending on the company they keep.

What this book does first then, is discuss some different facets of combining wine and food. I have tried to do more than just list what wine goes with what food. Over the years, I have developed some ideas about the how's and why's of matching wine and food. They have resulted partly from my academic training in food science and partly from analyzing the hundreds of suppers, lunches and tastings I have experienced in the past few years. Hopefully, these matchmaking principles will establish a set of guidelines, something you might call a framework, to which you can apply any gastronomic situation. It should enable you to make your own decisions about what wine goes with what food and not be bound to any outdated or otherwise unsuitable suggestions.

That brings me to an important point, namely to always trust your own judgement about what you like and what you don't like. Likes and dislikes are very personal things and no one can take them away from you. So no matter what is said in this or any other book about any particular wine or food, remember that you are always entitled to disagree. Trust yourself and don't be afraid to experiment!

To give you an idea of how generations of people all over the world have treated wine and food, I have devoted a portion of the book to a gastronomic tour of some well known wine regions. The areas reviewed represent places I have visited and come to understand by meeting wine growers, talking to chefs and eating at small, local restaurants. What you will see surfacing so often is the way that different circumstances of geography, culture and resources have led to the development of tremendously varied cuisines, yet all possessing a common reverence for wine and food.

No book on wine and food would be complete without a section on how to put it all together on a practical level. The third section of the book therefore begins by discussing "nutritious gastronomy" or how to eat and drink well yet still stay slim! It continues with a chapter on cooking with wine and finishes with a section on menu planning, with some sample menus that are sure to make you hungry!

To satisfy that hunger, a collection of my favourite recipes, all Taveroff originals, have been included in the last part of the book. They range from appetizers to desserts. Most are easy and quick. All are outstandingly delicious.

So read on and enjoy. Think and be stimulated. Dream of that great gourmet dinner. Then follow your dreams!

My sincere thanks...

To Hans, for introducing me to the world of wine and teaching me the basics of tasting in a way that no one else could ever do.

To Alan and Louise, for their excellent wine tastings that have provided me with a wealth of first hand experience and the kind of knowledge one cannot find in books.

To Nicole, for the kind advice and encouragement she has given to me on so many occasions.

To JWS, for believing that I had something to say and providing me with the opportunity to write it all down.

To Kenneth Christie, M.W., for his able assistance in preparing the chapter on grape types and the body-sweetness charts.

To Judy, Bart, Barbara, Shirley, Lidia and Elizabeth whose expertise and hard work were instrumental in converting my messy manuscript into the reality of a book.

And to my husband, for his untiring moral support, his proofreading, his knowledge, his compliments (and criticisms), and his willingness to eat absolutely any new thing I cook!

Arlene Taveroff

CONTENTS

PART I

THE HOW'S AND WHY'S
OF
MATCHING
WINES & FOODS

THE CLASSICS

The marriage of wine and food tends to put people into one of three camps. In the first are those who "play the field" and match any wine with any food. After all, as long as you like what you are doing, anything goes. Why limit yourself to traditional rules? In the second group are those who are much more timid. They hesitate to make any matches at all , thinking 'who are they' to make such important deicisions? If only there were a Yenta the Matchmaker in the world of food and wine! Then, there are the wine and food snobs who think they know it all and insist on doing everything the right way... "But darling, you simply MUST serve caviar with your Champagne (Brut, of course!)." Why this is so, they haven't a clue. So if they should run out of caviar (heaven forbid!) they have no idea what to substitute.

As you can see, there are dangers to each of these groups. Haphazard pairing can lead to either bliss or disaster. Relying on others to make your matches enables you to blame someone else for gastronomic disasters but can lead to them nonetheless. By following the snobby crowd you stand to miss a lot.

All this can be avoided by *understanding* the reasons behind wine and food matchups. Understanding enables you to make your own decisions and be intelligent and creative, all at the same time. Odd as it may seem, we can start by looking at some of the "classics" of the trendy crowd. Some of the more popular ones are:

Brut Champagne with Caviar

Médoc with Game

Côte de Nuits Burgundy with Roast Beef

Sauternes with Roquefort

Vintage Port with Stilton

Chablis with Oysters

Swiss Neufchâtel with Cheese Fondue

Retsina with Moussaka

Sauternes with Foie Gras (in Bordeaux)

Tokay d'Alsace with Foie Gras (in Alsace)

Muscat or Gewürztraminer with Muenster Cheese

Fino (sherry) with Olives (in Jerez)

Pauillac with Lamb

Gewürztraminer with Smoked Fish or Cheese

Sancerre with Chèvre

The first thing you might notice is that many of these combinations are foods and wines that come from the same region of a country or province. In other words, they naturally coexist together. For instance, lamb is raised around Pauillac, and olive trees grow everywhere in the south of Spain near Jerez. In fact, most classic combinations are based on regional resources and generations of local wisdom, handed down from generation to generation until they get to the point of being "common knowledge" or "local custom."

Remember, in past decades, travel and commerce were not the factors they are today. So the food of any region was necessarily accompanied by a wine that was locally available. Some say that growing in similar soil and climate gives the wine and the food a common mineral composition and therefore compatible tastes. Others rely on generations of local cuisine, and the gradual evolution of food preparation to suit and enhance the wines of the area. In any case, "local" was the keyword for both wine and food.

As an example, a Parisian gourmet at the turn of the century may have pronounced, in his or her wisdom, that roast beef should be served with a Côte de Nuits. It's true that both the strength and the quality of flavour in these two match very well. It may have been at that time, with that chef's choice of available wines, that the Côte de Nuits with roast beef was not only a good choice but the best choice. But today things are different. The world has become smaller. More is available. So while we know that roast beef still marries well with beef and burgundy, we can afford to be creative and untraditional, and to consider the possibilities of a Rioja, a Barolo, or a California Pinot Noir. In other words, as our world expands, so do our choices.

It is obvious that traditional choices based on regionality, although valid, are limiting. Some basic concepts of tasting and some underlying how to's and why's are necessaryto expand your horizons.

THE PERCEPTION OF FLAVOUR

Now you're probably finding yourself in one of three positions: a) you're delighted by the idea of needing to understand the why's and how's of wine and food match-ups; b) you think it's a lot of hogwash and you want to get to the bottom line; c) you're not sure — you need more input; or d) other. (Isn't that always the last choice?)

Regardless of which category you fit into, read on. If you're an "a," you will find yourself being led through a group of logical concepts based on real life experiences, all easy to apply to new situations. If you're a "b," feel free to skim through all that, just like you do with a financial report, and you *will* reach the bottom line; namely some specific dos and don'ts, and some concrete ideas on how to select your wines. If you're a "c" or "d," then perhaps further reading is just what you need to take a stand. Let's start by discussing taste itself.

The receptors for taste stimuli are "taste buds." Most of our taste buds are located on the upper surface of the tongue, especially at its tip, sides and back.

Each taste bud is composed of a group of cells — from two to twelve in number, arranged like the staves of a barrel. On the tip of each cell there are microscopic hair-like projections which extend from a pore in the skin. The average person has over nine thousand of these taste buds in the mouth. They are constantly degenerating and regenerating. However, as we get older, there is more of the former and less of the latter going on — which is why older people tend to lose some of their taste acuity.

Not all taste buds are created equal! Different groups of taste buds are more sensitive to certain types of taste and less sensitive to others. Those at the back of the tongue are especially sensitive to bitterness. Those at the tip of the tongue are best able to detect sweetness. Sourness is best noticed by taste buds on the sides of the tongue. Sensitivity to salt is about the same on all areas of the tongue.

A person's response to a wine or food is influenced by its temperature. Sensitivity to sweet and sour generally increases with a rise in temperature. So a dessert wine that is ice cold will not seem as sweet as it does after it warms up a little. If the wine had any bitterness when it was very cold, this will seem to diminish as the wine warms up. That's because sensitivity to bitterness decreases with an increase in temperature.

Whatever the temperature, some combination of those four basic tastes will be perceived by the taste buds. Nerve cells from the taste buds carry messages to the brain, where a judgement is made about the nature of the stimulus (food or wine). Here memories and analogies come into play, so when we describe a food or a wine, it is not only in terms of the four basic tastes. It also depends on the particular experiences that have been stored in the brain of the taster.

Nevertheless, the four basic tastes are worth considering in a bit more detail.

SOURNESS is the simplest taste. It is sometimes called "acidity," for it is activated by acids, both organic and inorganic. Specifically, it is the hydrogen ions that produce a sour (or acidic) taste. The more there are, the more sour (or acidic) the solution.

Acidity in wine is a rather complex notion. Generally, acidity gives wine a certain liveliness, much the same as a twist of lemon does to fish. With the right amount of acidity a wine is refreshing and interesting. With too much it is disagreeably tart, and with too little it is flat and flabby.

The organic acids such as malic, lactic, citric and tartaric produce the acidic taste in wine and it is the particular balance of acids present that influences the overall impression. Some attack the palate immediately; others more slowly. Some have a clean, mouth-cleansing character, while others have an unpleasant aspect to them.

SWEETNESS is a taste activated by sugars. However, there are other substances, chemically quite different from sugars, that also elicit a sweet sensation. In wines, the major ingredient involved in sweetness is the amount of residual sugar left after fermentation. Apart from this, the glycerol and alcohol also contribute but to a lesser degree. Sweetness tends to add weight or intensity to a wine, enabling it to stand up to rich or strongly flavoured foods.

SALTINESS is the taste elicited by ordinary table salt and is a taste sensation seldom encountered in wine. Some sherries, however, have a slightly salty taste — especially those made from grapes grown near the sea.

BITTERNESS refers to a taste which is slow in developing and is usually noticed at the back of the mouth. It does *not* refer to that fuzzy, drying sensation you sometimes experience on the tongue and cheeks. That is a mouthfeel, called astringency. Bitterness is the longest lasting of the four basic tastes, probably due to the great affinity that bitter compounds have for the taste buds at the rear of the tongue. In food, many substances cause a bitter sensation. Common ones are caffeine, nicotine and quinine. In wines, both bitterness and astringency tend to result from a high level of tannins.

Except in the laboratory, none of these four tastes occur in isolation. In real life, the four basic tastes mingle with odour and memories to form a mixture of sensations that bombard us more or less simultaneously.

This can be mighty confusing! Dr. Michael O'Mahony illustrates the point very well in an article called *How we Perceive Flavour* published in *Nutrition Today,* May/June 1984. He has the reader look at Fraser's spiral, which you see below. You probably see a spiral, right? Wrong! It's actually a set of concentric circles. Prove it to yourself by tracing a coloured pencil around one of the circles. Amazing isn't it? When you look at the figure the messages about the background (the diamonds) and messages about the foreground (the circles) are interfering with each other. One carries information about direction, the other about orientation. The two together form an integrated, but in this case, incorrect perception.

Similar interactions occur with taste and smell, as well as with taste and colour. Distortion even occurs when you are faced with two different tastes (e.g. salty and sweet) at the same time.

The interaction between colour and taste is an interesting phenomenon to experience. For one thing, colour gives important clues as to what a food or wine will taste like. It presents us with a set of expectations. A platter of meat, carefully arranged with visual appeal will transmit the positive message that it must taste delicious! The same meat, very dark in colour and plunked on a plate, will lead to totally different expectations. This is no truer than with wine tasting. Both the nature and the amount of colour in a wine tell all kinds of stories, and build up expectations as to what to expect in the mouth. What is interesting is how often the palate confirms the expectations set up by the eye; partly because there is often a correlation, and partly because our minds play tricks on us.

Next time you have a group of wine snobs over, try pouring some cheap plonk into a bottle bearing the label of a fine wine. (You must first have invested in the fine wine — and drunk it.) Show the bottle and the label when you serve it, saying you opened it ahead of time to let it breathe. Ask for comments and, unless your friends are experienced tasters, I'd be willing to bet that most will rant and rave about the great wine.

Seriously, though, it is important to acknowledge the role of visual clues in tasting both wine and food. I once had to identify the flavour of a blue-coloured pudding. After three wrong guesses (and feeling quite foolish) I was told it was strawberry. The moral of the story — don't eat blue pudding? Not really. The point I'm trying to make is that mixed up messages mix up the brain. When you have two different inputs coming in to the brain at the same time, the resulting perception is often ''altered.''

As I have mentioned, this even happens when you mix the four basic tastes (which you do all the time when you eat and drink). One example is the inter-action between sweetness and saltiness. The perception of saltiness is reduced in the presence of sugar. This could be due to messages about salt being inhibited by messages about sugar, or vice versa. Or it could also be a blending effect. Either way, the brain takes all the inputs and by some magic and mysterious process, sorts out the conflicts. The resulting impressions are interesting because they are usually distortions of reality. The trick is to understand the distortions and make them work for you rather than against you. That is really what is behind wine and food match-ups; playing with perceptions.

The how to's will come in the next chapter. First let me explain another basic tasting concept called adaptation. Adaptation is a mechanism which ensures that the brain constantly has room for new information. (Why tie it up with old news?) In other words, the brain perceives changes but does not perceive the lack of change.

To put it simply, your taste buds can handle only so much at one time. Each stimulus, after all, needs to be "processed" through a taste bud where it triggers a nerve impulse to the brain (at which point a judgement is made about the nature of that stimulus). There are a finite number of taste buds in the mouth and each stimulus "processing" requires a finite length of time. So with too much of one stimulus, a "backlog" is created and you temporarily lose your ability to perceive that stimulus.

Interpose a second, different type of taste, and the situation changes. Each different taste excites different taste buds. So while the first set is "recovering" from its excitement, the second set in in action. By the time the second set is "tired," the first set is ready again.

The phenomenon of adaption is especially noticeable in perceptions of odour. You come in from a cold, wintry day and notice the smell of your favourite soup. You stay in and relax and very soon the smell of the soup has gone. In actual fact, the smell hasn't disappeared, the nerve impulses about it have simply weakened. Your nose has adapted to the odour.

You have to keep working to change what you smell, otherwise everything goes dead. For example, picture yourself enjoying a glass of your favourite wine. It's absolutely delightful for a few minutes. Then the bouquet disappears and your enjoyment becomes based on the memory of that first moment more than anything else. It's the same with food. Too much of one thing will cause even the best dish to become boring and tiresome. But alternate the two, the food with the wine, and the adaptation poblem never surfaces. You're constantly registering change. Stimulus strength never dies. The food enhances your perception of the wine, and the wine enhances your perception of the food.

Have you ever noticed that when your nose is stuffed, food seems tasteless? That's right – odour is an important component of flavour. So once your nose adapts to the odour of a food or wine, you lose not only the (hopefully) pleasant aroma but also some of the taste.

To make matters worse, as O'Mahony points out, the phenomenon of adaptation also affects your taste receptors. Initially the taste receptors on your tongue are at "zero level" for a particular taste, let's say sweetness. Now taste something sweet. The sweet receptors register this as sweet since it is different from the sweetness you had in your mouth originally, which was zero. Now keep drinking the same solution. After a while, it's not that sweet after all! Why? Your sweetness receptors have adapted and in effect they are "re-zeroed." Your standard of comparison is changed so anything you taste now will be compared not to the original "true zero" standard, but to the "new zero." Sound abstract?

9

Here is a way of giving the concept some substance:

TRY THE FOLLOWING EXPERIMENT: (Come on - really do it!)

(A) EFFECT OF SOUR: Take two small glasses of tap water (not too cold). Into one, add the juice of a lemon. Drink some of the plain water first. Note its taste, if any. Next, drink some of the treated water and note its taste. Then immediately go back to the plain water. Has its taste changed? (If so, how?)

notes _____

_____

(B) EFFECT OF SWEET: Repeat the above but treat one glass of plain water with two teaspoons of sugar (instead of lemon).

notes _____

_____

(C) EFFECT OF SALT: Repeat again, this time treating one glass with 1 teaspoon of salt.

notes _____

_____

Although everybody's reaction is different, what most people notice from this experiment is the following:

Initially, the water has no noticeable taste.
A. After the sour water, the plain water appears somewhat *sweet*.
B. After the sweet water, the plain water appears somewhat *bitter*.
C. After the salty water, the plain water appears somewhat *sour and bitter*.

Go back and repeat the experiment with these conclusions in mind!

Just in case you are thinking that I'm getting lost on a sidestreet, remember that it's these sensations of sour, sweet, salty and bitter that you are dealing with every time you eat and drink! What you have just learned is absolutely relevant to food and wine. For instance, have you ever had a sweet dessert served with a Brut Champagne? And you thought you didn't like the Champagne because it was bitter? Now you know it wasn't the Champagne per se, it was the sweet dessert accompanying it that was really at fault! For just as in the water experiments above, a sweet tasting food makes the wine following it seem more bitter than normal. So if Champagne is to be served with dessert, make sure that the sweetness of the wine and the food match!

Have you ever wondered why many books suggest that you avoid wine with Chinese food? The reasons for this are many but one should now be obvious. If the Chinese food is salty, as many Chinese dishes are, the wine will seem somewhat sour and bitter next to it! Just like in the salty water experiment.

The sour water experiment applies too; remember how it made the plain water seem sweet. How about using this to your advantage? Drink a fairly acidic wine with seafood and notice the results; the seafood will never have tasted so sweet! Yes, the acidity (or sourness) of the wine will have emphasized the sweetness of the seafood, giving it that fresh, from the ocean taste!

One further word should be said about sweet and sour. The combination is frequently found in everything from Jewish meatballs to German wine. There is an important and even vital balance to keep between sweet and sour or sugar and acid, as it is often described. Sugar reduces sourness. So a dry German Riesling (there aren't too many!) is often unpleasant in its acidity. Unbalanced is actually a better word than unpleasant. The taste seems only sour, with nothing on the other side of the teeter totter. Leave some residual sugar in the same wine and its high acidity is perceived differently. It is no longer as sour, no longer unpleasant or unbalanced. The sugar and acid balance each other out, with the sugar reducing the perception of sourness.

Knowing this, you can enhance a slightly too acid wine by combining it with a somewhat sweet food. The sweetness of the food will reduce the sourness you perceive in the wine; the sourness or acidity of the wine, in turn, will enhance the sweetness of the food. Each makes the other better!

It should be apparent now that the basic tastes of sweet, sour, salt and bitterness permeate all types of wine and food. In addition, there are appearance, aroma and mouthfeel, all of which play on your senses, more or less together, to give the overall impression of flavour. The interactions between these components form the basis of meaningful wine and food matchmaking.

MATCHING FOOD AND WINE
A Word About Tannins

One of the most interesting interactions between wine and food involves tannins. The presence of tannins in a wine leaves a sensation of dryness on the tongue and palate. This sensation, called astringency, is a mouthfeel, not a taste. Tannins do have a taste however, usually recognized by a slow developing but very distinct bitterness, most often felt at the back of the tongue.

One way of dealing with a tannic wine is to put it away for a few years. With bottle age, tannins gradually precipitate out to form a fine sediment. Once you decant the wine to get rid of this sediment, you are left with a wine in which bitterness and astringency are remarkably reduced. The fruit and other qualities can then begin to shine.

However, this is not the only way to skin the cat! A more immediate method involves the use of food. Clever matching of wine with food can change your perception of a tannic, young wine quite drastically. What is behind this art of wine/food matchmaking is science; chemistry, to be exact. But don't panic; you need not be a chemistry major to understand this. Just think for a minute of a cup of strong plain tea or better yet, try some. Notice its astringent, drying feel in your mouth, and its bitterness. Now add a good dose of milk to the tea and try it again. Those astringent and bitter qualities have decreased noticeably. Why? The protein in the milk has reacted with the tannins in the tea, tying some of them up and rendering them useless.

With wine and food, it's the same thing. Protein in food effectively reduces the level of tannins in wine. This is especially true when you cook with wine and there is an intimate and prolonged contact between the wine and the protein, as in a meat with wine sauce or a stew. That is why you often hear people suggesting the use of a young wine for cooking; the tannins don't matter because they "cook out," so to speak.

When you eat a protein food like meat or cheese or pâté, the same thing happens. Even though you're taking the wine and food into your mouth in sequence, enough cheese is left over in your mouth after you swallow that the wine changes and mellows. As a result, the fruit and other qualities of the wine are able to come to the forefront and the wine seems improved and enhanced – all because of the food.

Wine merchants take advantage of this and often serve cheese with the wine they are selling you. So you see, they're not doing this out of the goodness of their hearts! They're making use of the fact that the cheese will enhance your perception of the wine! The expression "Buy on an apple, sell on cheese" now makes sense. Amazing? That's only the beginning! Let's see what else wine and food can do to each other.

The Role of Body

The body of a wine just like that of a man or woman, can vary considerably, ranging from thin and lightweight to big and heavy. Food also has this property and can range from light and delicate to heavy and robust. What food goes with what wine is partly dependent on relative weights. Mutt and Jeff partnerships are generally undesirable. Whether it's a big wine with delicate food, or a delicate wine with heavy food, the result is the same. One is overpowered, squashed and unappreciated. So it is vital to match "body types" when matching food and wine.

The practice of drinking Médoc wines with game is a good example. Most types of game have a very pronounced flavour. If accompanied by a light wine, the flavour of the meat dominates to the extent of overpowering the wine. A full-bodied, assertive Médoc, on the other hand, would stand up to the meat and contribute its fair share to the gastronomic partnership.

Other classic combinations can also be explained through the concept of body. Pauillac and lamb, Tokay d'Alsace and foie gras, Gewürztraminer and smoked fish and many more all have similar body weights as the basis of their marriage.

You may have noticed or read that different fish and seafood dishes require different wines. This too, is based on body, which is determined partly by the fish itself, and partly by the method of preparation. So a delicate dish like poached sole would go well with a light, crisp wine like Muscadet. Add a rich sauce, as for instance in Sole Normande or Sole Mornay and the wine needs to have more body to balance the cream. Hence a more full-bodied white, such as a Chardonnay would be suitable. If the fish itself is fairly fatty and full-flavoured, like salmon or trout, it is particularly important that the wine have enough acid and flavour to stand up to it. Remember that a creamy or fatty food makes a wine seem less acid than if drunk on its own. An Alsatian Riesling would do well because of its rich flavour and high acidity.

While on the subject of fat and acid, it should be stressed that as the fat content of a food increases, so does its heaviness and its mouthcoating action. Both these qualities can breed fatigue very quickly. Herein lies another reason for drinking a high acid wine with a highly fatty dish. The acidity of the wine is lively. It has a wakening effect, providing a refreshing contrast to the smooth, heavy fat of the food. The wine therefore acts as a counterbalance, preventing the fatigue which would result from unvarying repetition of only one sensation in the mouth.

The wine's strength of taste or flavour should depend on the food. The stronger the taste of the food, the more robust and assertive the wine needs to be. The more delicate the food, the more subtle the wine. For example, roast duck, with its strong gamey flavour, requires an assertive, full-bodied red, like Côte Rôtie or Hermitage. Veal, in a cream sauce would be overpowered by either of these, but would be complemented nicely by a delicate but lively white wine, like an Alsatian Riesling, or an Italian Soave, or Frascati.

We can now see that the concept of body or weight also lies behind those classic rules of red wine with meats like beef and lamb; either with veal, pork and game; white with chicken. These matches have little to do with colour. What's really being matched is weight in the mouth. Beef and lamb are simply heavier meats than chicken, possessing more definite flavour. They would tend to over-power a white wine. Chicken, on the other hand is light, and subtle enough in taste to enhance, rather than mask, a white wine. Depending on its preparation, it can support a variety of different wines, ranging all the way from the light and crisp to the more powerful and full-bodied. At times, a light red is even in order! For instance, a dish like Chicken Parmesan, in which chicken breasts are coated with tomato sauce and cheese, calls for a light red like Valpolicella or Bardolino. Coq au Riesling will naturally demand the same wine used in the recipe, namely a crisp Alsatian Riesling which is perfect in this case because the high acidity of the wine is needed to counterbalance the smooth, rich creaminess of the sauce. Other recipes, like Chicken in Cheese Sauce need a more full-bodied wine to hold up to the flavour of the cheeses. The exact choice of wine would depend on which cheeses went into the sauce, but could vary from Alsatian Muscat to Italian Chianti.

Preparation is important in the "in between" meats. Veal, rabbit and pork can take either a red or a white wine depending on the nature of the ingredients in the cooking. If a wine is used in the cooking, then that wine, or a similar one, should be drunk with the meal. So Veal Marsala would go nicely with a glass of very dry Marsala or a red wine like Montepulciano. Prepared with a spicy tomato sauce, or with ham and cheese, a fuller red is in order; perhaps a Chianti Classico, a Sassicaia or a Barolo. There are many possibilities, but the concept is always the same; the weight of the wine must match the weight of the food, and vice versa. In other words, body and weight are measured *relative* to the accompanying food or drink.

Relativity Revisited

The concept of relativity is crucial in wine and food matchmaking. In fact, I often wonder if Einstein was really thinking of wine when he proposed that "everything is relative." (Probably not, but the concept *does* apply to the gourmet world.)

This became apparent to me one evening at dinner. I was preparing a potful of bouillabaisse and chilling a bottle of Tavel to serve with it. One of my guests looked at me, rather perplexed, and asked why I was serving a rosé with fish when a white wine was traditional. My first reaction was, "Rosé is traditional with bouillabaisse," and I immediately started in on a long blurb about regional wines with regional foods. However, deep down, I knew there was more to it than that. Why did a Tavel suit the dish and not a white?

Being a somewhat impulsive, "let's try it" kind of person, I got a bottle of Montagny from my cellar and chilled it. We sat down to dinner with a glass of Montagny and of course, the bouillabaisse. Everyone tasted the wine first, making comments on their impressions and then continued with a few mouthfuls of food, followed by more wine. Lo and behold, there was the answer! The Montagny, so assertive and full of varietal character when tasted on its own, now seemed thin and weak. Next to the food the wine had changed completely. The taste of the bouillabaisse had overpowered it, making it seem thin and characterless in comparison.

So the taste of the wine is certainly not a constant. It can change – or at least appear to change – depending on its company. Everything (as the saying goes) is relative. The taste of any wine or food is automatically compared to what preceded it, and is perceived in light of that comparison.

Yes, that was the real reason why I had chosen the Tavel over a white wine. It would have the body and the strength needed to stand up to the hearty provençal fish stew. With bated breath we opened the Tavel and found just that.

The wine and the food married beautifully as though they were made for each other.

That evening made me aware that the concept of relativity is absolutely basic to the art of tasting. In fact, I realized that the idea follows quite logically from the principle of adaptation, and applies to food as well as wine. Consider an apple, for instance. By itself it tastes like an apple. There is some sensation of sweet and some of sour. How much depends largely on your memory of previous apples. But nevertheless, a certain taste is perceived. Now put down the apple and swallow some lemon juice (gulp!) and then taste the apple again. It will appear more sweet and less sour than before. Why? Because your standard of comparison is no longer previous apples, but that sour lemon juice! The apple hasn't changed, only your perception of it. Similarly, if you swallow a spoonful of something sweet like maple syrup, and then try the apple again, the apple will taste more sour and less sweet than it did before. Once again, the taste of the food is governed by what has preceded it in your mouth.

The concept of relativity can work for or against you. I recently found it working against me when I was put in the position of having to drink an Alsatian Gewürztraminer with a veal dish smothered in cream sauce. The wine, tasted by itself, was very dry and highly acidic with a distinctly spicy note. The food was mild, creamy and delicate. Alone each was a wonderful taste experience. Together they told a different story. What happened was that the mild cream sauce made the Gewürztraminer seem even more spicy than it was when tasted alone. The Gewürztraminer, in turn, made the veal with its sauce seem not just mild but tasteless and bland. The contrast between the wine and the food polarized the two, making what were essentially good features appear bad.

However that need not be the case. You can turn the whole concept around to your advantage with just a little planning. The trick is to choose foods and wines that enhance each other and mask, rather than make obvious, any faults. For instance, suppose you have in front of you a red Mercurey that seems overly acidic when tasted alone. Serve it with a tart cheese dip – it will attune your mouth to tartness and make the Mercurey seem less so, thus increasing your enjoyment of the wine.

The concept of relativity helps to explain many of the classic do's and don'ts of the wine and food world.

For instance you probably know that anybody with any *savoir faire* at all does not drink a wine with a vinaigrette dressed salad. Now you also know why. Relative to the acidity of the dressing, even the most well balanced wine is going to appear flabby and weak. The same thing happens when you put a wine against tomatoes, citrus fruit or juice, gazpacho, or any vegetable marinated in a vinaigrette. The high acidity of these foods overpowers the wine, making it seem flat and lacking in liveliness. This in turn, makes the food seem even more acidic and biting than it already is and a vicious cycle is created.

In the case of spicy foods the story is similar. The strong flavour of dishes like chili, curry or some Chinese food is nearly impossible to match in a wine. Even the most full-bodied wines will seem thin next to these dishes. In fact the heat and the staying power of these foods requires a fire brigade more than anything else. Water, beer or plonk of any kind will suffice. Or you may wish to try something so different that there is no competition.

Relativity also explains why you don't usually drink a dry wine with a sweet dessert. The wine will seem overly tart next to the dessert and create a kind of "taste shock" in your mouth as you switch from dessert to wine and back again. The food and the drink are in totally different ballparks. No matter how refreshing the wine may be it will strike out. What is needed is a wine with enough acidity to be refreshing, and enough sweetness to be in the same league as the dessert. So depending on the specific dessert, a wine such as a German Auslese might be suitable, or perhaps a French Sauternes.

When enjoying cheese at the end of a meal, be careful. Cheese and wine are reputed to go together beautifully but not every cheese goes well with every wine. Once again relativity helps to explain which do and which don't. Always stay at the same level, especially with regard to acidity and taste intensity. So don't eat a blue cheese with a delicate white wine unless you want to knock over the wine. Pick something with more body or more intensity, such as port. In the case of other cheeses and other wines, the choices may be different, but the principle stays the same.

The key issue – whether you're talking about cheese or anything else – is that you cannot treat eating and drinking as two separate events. Instead they must be seen as two parts of a single activity, interacting with each other to produce a total taste experience.

How to Combat Fatigue

The idea of adaptation was discussed earlier as being a basic problem in tasting, insofar as it resets our tastebuds and makes a once pleasurable stimulus less perceptible.

At this point it might be a good idea to look at this in a bit more detail, and begin to examine some possible solutions. Suppose you're enjoying that special wine. Each mouthful excites pretty well the same taste buds. Too much too fast creates a backlog. You drink but don't taste and you sniff, but don't smell. Your taste buds (and olfactory receptors) have become temporarily desensitized and fatigued. They need a break that only time will bring. Drinking slowly will work as will sniffing, then taking a break before sniffing again. But this style of stop and start drinking can be difficult. There must be another way.

The answer lies in alternating sensations. Marry a wine with a food that uses different taste buds and let each mouthful of food and wine give some taste buds a rest. For example, consider the combination of lamb and Rioja. The Rioja has a certain amount of acidity (depending, of course, on the particular wine and its age) and the lamb has hardly any. The Rioja has a certain amount of sweetness derived from the glycerol, the ethanol, and trace amounts of residual sugar; the lamb does not. So each bite of food and wine excites different taste buds, providing a constantly changing, and therefore exciting, taste experience.

A recent experience illustrates this especially well. I was cooking a dish of spicy Szechwan Shrimp. The only cold wine available was a Yugoslavian Traminer, a medium-bodied white, somewhat sweet, with a distinctly peachy note and a hint of spice. Interesting, I thought. I tried it and was amazed! The shrimps were spicy and salty, while the wine was semisweet and mellow. What I discovered was that the wine was powerful enough to hold its own against the shrimp, yet it had the effect of going to the country on the weekend; it was serene and calming. A welcome change after a mouthful of the food, which was more like the work week; exciting and stimulating. Alternating the two made each a welcome treat. There was never too much of a good thing.

By the way, too much of a good thing is exactly what happens when you try tasting wine after a citrus fruit. The fruit contains so much acid that your taste buds for acid become overloaded and disfunctional. So when you taste the wine, its acidity, although present, is not perceived. That explains why here acidity of the wine seems low relative to the citrus fruit and also why if you interpose a biscuit between the fruit and wine, the situation improves dramatically. The biscuit has no acidity whatsoever, so your taste buds have the chance to recuperate before you drink the wine.

Recuperated taste buds are ready for action. That explains further some of the situations discussed under the idea of relativity. If you recall, I discussed how drinking a Gewürztraminer with Veal in Cream Sauce accentuated both the spiciness of the wine and the blandness of the food resulting in a bad combination. The reason for this should now be apparent. The wine and the food were so completely different in their taste characteristics, that taste bud recovery was complete. In this case however, it was excessive (at least for my taste). The moral of the story is: plan intelligently. Fatigue is not a weakness. Rather, it needs to be considered an aspect of tasting, that, like other aspects, can enhance the pleasure you experience from food and wine.

Finish: Foods Have it Too

In wine tasting circles we often talk about the finish of a wine. Briefly, it refers to the sensations of taste, odour and touch that remain in the mouth after a wine is swallowed. One expert I know calls it a "souvenir" left by the wine to the taster. The finer the wine, the longer, the more identifiable and more complex is the aftertaste or finish.

Most wine lovers know this, but stop there; which is understandable since wine is their frame of reference. However, this need not be the case. As a wine taster and a cook, I usually think of both wine and food. It's actually quite fascinating to apply wine tasting concepts to food.

The concept of finish and length is a perfect example. Some foods, once swallowed, are gone from both the palate and the memory, leaving no impression. Others stay, but are mild and linger only briefly before vanishing. Some tastes loiter, remaining for a time in the mouth. In any case, the message is the same. Foods have the qualities of "finish" and "length," just as wines do. Let's take a look at some foods in light of these properties.

The finish of a food exerts an important influence on a wine. When the taste of a food lingers in your mouth and/or has a dominating or unusual flavour with respect to the wine, the taste of the food persists when you sip the wine. At the instant the wine hits your palate, you forget that the flavour comes from the food. You think you are identifying the taste of the wine. Your impression is that the wine tastes strange. In actual fact, the wine has taken on some of the characteristics of the food.

For instance, if you ever try to eat a blue cheese with a light, delicate white wine, the wine will taste sour and mouldy. Similarly, a delicate white wine tasted after a mouthful of asparagus tends to acquire a definite vegetal note. Most wines tasted after a mint sauce will taste minty. And so the examples could go on and on.

The way to combat this tendency is to choose a wine that has enough "umph" to fight back. In other words, the wine must have enough character and intensity to assert itself on the palate, even in the presence of residual food taste. At this point, the concept of relativity starts to intermingle with the idea of finish. Remember, intensity is relative to what came before.

So far, our approach has been from the point of view of food first, and how the lingering taste of the food affects the wine which follows. That's not the only way to do it. From the other side of the fence, it becomes apparent that the finish of a wine also needs to be considered in any wine and food matchmaking. Given that a wine has a certain finish, what food would follow it best?

If the wine is extremely short, leaving little or no lingering aftertaste, then it hardly matters. Almost any food will be suitable because there is no aftertaste which the food can interfere with. In fact, this would be a good place for a mild, bland dish.

If, on the other hand, the wine has a very definite and long finish, more planning is required. For instance, the finish of some California Chardonnays is quite long and oaky. If followed by a very mild and delicate food, such as Poached Sole, the fish would take on some of the oaky aftertaste and lose the subtleties it would otherwise have offered. A more strongly flavoured food would provide better balance.

You can use the concept of finish purposefully to give a food or wine some of the characteristics of the other. For example if you want to accentuate the nuttiness of Emmental cheese, pair it with a sherry. If you want to strengthen the gamey taste of a roast duck, team it with a Chelois which has a slightly toasty and ''wild'' flavour, and so on, depending on the feature you want to accentuate.

There are times when the taste and the finish of a wine are so outstanding, so enjoyable, that you don't want anything to interfere. All you want is to enjoy the wine. In this case you might decide to drink the wine alone. The Germans do this frequently with their Beerenauslese and Trockenbeerenauslese. You might decide to get together with some friends and enjoy the wine in a tasting format. If food is to be had with the wine, you would probably want to plan a dish whose taste supports and shows off the wine without dominating it. An apricot tart is one of my favourite accompaniments to Beerenauslese. The sweetness of the two match well, as does their richness (Furthermore, the acidity of the wine is a refreshing counterbalance to the fat in the pastry). But more than that, their flavours and aftertastes harmonize and support each other.

So it's really a two way street. The wine and the food both tend to linger in the mouth. Each has an effect on the other possibly in the direction of detracting or overpowering, but with some planning, in the direction of mutual enhancement.

Balance and Harmony

The concept of fatigue led us to the idea of alternating taste sensations and avoiding too much repetition so as to keep as many taste buds as possible active and functioning. It sounds reasonable, and, in fact, is. But it's not simple.

With what, for example, do you alternate the wine? Something "opposite?" That could mean mixing a spicy wine with a non-spicy food. Or a sweet food with a dry, acidic wine. Or a heavy food with a light wine. The possibilities are endless if you think only of opposites. The trouble is, some opposites work and some don't such as in the first suggestion (a spicy wine with a non-spicy food). For example, a peppery Zinfandel will provide a pleasant contrast to a bland steak. However, a spicy Gewürztraminer could completely destroy a delicate fish dish. The second example, of a sweet food with a dry wine, will usually not work either. The reason is that the sweetness of the food will bring out any bitterness in the wine and make it more noticeable. If in doubt, see how *Tarte au Sucre* goes with that leftover Muscadet or Chablis. As for heavy food with light wine, the Germans often argue it is desirable in that wine refreshes the palate. In Germany you see people drinking Riesling with everything from sausages to venison. I find that you must plan carefully, for more often than not, a light wine will be overpowered by a heavy food.

Alternating taste sensations is therefore more complicated than you might first presume. It's not just a matching of opposites. You must also remember the concepts of relativity and finish already discussed. All of these ideas come together in the real life situation of tasting, and all act concurrently. In other words a food and a wine should excite different taste buds in order to avoid fatigue, but their taste and their intensity should still be relative so that neither is overpowered. The latter applies to both the time that the food is in the mouth and after it is swallowed.

For example, I was once served a dish of scallops in a lemony butter sauce. The scallops were tender and sweet, while the sauce was tart but rich. These tastes, the sweet, the tart and the buttery, lingered in the mouth for a deliciously long time before fading. The wine served with this dish was a California Chardonnay. Theoretically it should have been a good match. Unfortunately, the wine was very light-bodied and lacked both varietal character and complexity. When tasted after the food, it took on a distinctly lemony note. The aftertaste of the scallop dish was stronger than the wine, so the taste of the wine was overpowered and became indistinguishable from the lemony aftertaste of the scallops. To make matters worse, the sweet taste of the scallops made the wine appear relatively dry and more lacking in fruit than it already was.

If the wine had possessed more character, it might have stood up to the food and held its own, balancing the flavour of the food with its own. But matching wine with a lemony taste is playing with dynamite. Lemon is one of those tastes that once in the mouth tends to linger and carry over into the next food or drink that comes along. No wine should taste of lemon! So perhaps a better solution would be to change the food. In this case, I would have omitted the lemon in the sauce, and added instead some Chardonnay reduced to intensify the flavour. The other alternative would have been to sauté the scallops in butter and serve them as simply as possible.

It really depends on whether you want to show off the wine or the food. If I have prepared a very special dish, with complex nuances of flavour, I might want to make it the centre of attraction. In that case, I would serve it with a suitable, but simple wine. If, on the other hand, I have a wine that I want to show off, then I would make sure that the food plays a supporting, rather than competing role. In each case the concept is the same; to balance something simple with something complex.

Balance is a somewhat abstract concept that sometimes means opposites and sometimes means sameness. It always means harmony. It's a little bit instinctive and therefore something you develop a gut feeling for after years of tasting experience. But in the meantime you need some guidelines.

Be careful with "sameness," for it could bring boredom or conflict. For instance, where a wine and a food share a feature so similar that neither stands out, neither occupies the center stage it deserves. On the other hand, a moderate amount of "sameness" provides a balance so your mouth doesn't go through culture shock every time you switch from wine to food and back again. For example if you try drinking a dry wine with a sweet dessert, your mouth goes crazy because the difference is too great. Your taste buds would rather fight than switch. A wine and a food must be relatively the same in some basic feature like sweetness or body before differences can be played with.

A classic example is that of Sauternes and Roquefort. The Sauternes is rich and sweet, and very smooth in the mouth. A good Sauternes will also have a decent amount of acidity, something you may not perceive as such owing to the sweetness. You only notice the good balance. The Roquefort seems completely different because it is salty, tangy and rather sharp and acidic in the mouth. Yet the Roquefort and Sauternes go well together since each has enough strength and assertiveness relative to the other to hold its own. The two also match in their acidity. So although the two seem different, they possess a basic underlying compatibility that permits the differences to act positively.

This brings us to the other side of the fence; the role of opposites in wine and food. One thing that opposites do is complete a gastronomic picture. It often happens that each component of a wine and food pair is incomplete by itself, but, with the other, forms a pleasing whole. Perhaps each partner counterbalances the weak points of the other, bringing out the best while hiding the faults.

For example, a wine and food with opposite mouthfeels will often complement each other very well. I recently tasted a 1979 St. Emilion (Château Canon LaGaffelière). Although it had plenty of fruit, its youthful astringency was very apparent on the palate. However, when tasted again after some rich, mouth-coating pâté my perception of the wine changed in that it seemed less tannic. The reason for this was that the pâté, with its high fat content and smooth mouthfeel, coated the mouth, offering a "cloak of protection" against the harsh tannins of the wine. While one coated the mouth, the other "scoured" it. Each in itself would have been tiring, but together counterbalanced each other and created a harmonious partnership.

In the case of spicy food, the situation is a bit more difficult. When discussing the concept of relativity I said that "the strong flavour of dishes like chili, curry and some Chinese food is nearly impossible to match in a wine." Don't panic, I'm not about to change my mind. I merely want to point out how the key word here is "nearly." Sometimes a mildly spicy dish will go well with a wine. For example, I have a Chinese Beef and Vegetables recipe that goes well with an old style woody Rioja. The Rioja possesses enough strength of flavour to stand up to the food. (Remember relativity.) Its depth and woodiness are somehow very appropriate as the weight of the wood smothers all those little spicy elves that dance in your mouth after swallowing the food.

In some ways, the Rioja and the Chinese food are the same with respect to intensity and strength of flavour so they obey the laws of relativity and finish. Yet at the same time they are different. In the mouth, one is rather hot and lively, while the other is quiet but pronounced and woody. Each has a quality the other lack. Fatigue is avoided and each taste is new and exciting, with the overall sensation being one of harmony and balance.

Balance. An interesting word, with a lot of meaning. It reminds me a bit of those old-fashioned scales that have one pan going up as the other goes down. You can't do anything to one side without affecting the other. It is the same with wine and food. Each affects the other and each makes a contribution to the total picture of your gastronomic experience. It is up to you to think and plan so that the components add up to create a pleasing picture.

APPLYING THE CONCEPTS
Using Your Knowledge

The last chapter introduced you to some very basic and very important concepts about matching food and wine. The following statements summarize the salient points that we discussed.

Match body types and taste intensities.

Fat reduces your perception of acidity. The balance between sweetness and acidity is also important in many wines and/or foods.

Everything is perceived relative to what preceded it.

Consider the aftertaste of food as well as wine when making matches.

Your senses are subject to fatigue. Change combats fatigue.

Food and wine unite to form a total gastronomic experience. Balance between these components is essential to a harmonious whole.

Understanding and remembering these few generalizations is more important (and easier) than memorizing long lists of specific suggestions.

However it's only the first step because the purpose of knowing these concepts is not to impress your friends with the knowledge per se, but to apply and use it. For example, the idea that fat reduces the perception of acidity has no intrinsic value in itself. Apply it to a meal, though, and it becomes invaluable. It tells you that the chicken in cream sauce is going to need a wine with enough acidity to not seem flat next to the food. Remember the Alsatian Riesling that seemed almost too puckery when tasted by itself? It might be just the right thing! You see it's not the knowledge that really counts, it's how you use it.

That's all very well and good – you most likely agree whole-heartedly at this point. But how do you do it? In order to apply the ideas you have just read and actually choose an appropriate wine for a given food, it's important to have a pretty good idea about the characteristics of different wines. Which are dry, which are medium dry, and which are sweet? Which are light, and which are full-bodied? What about their acidity and their fruitiness? These are important things to know. The best way to find out, of course, and the most delightful, is to taste and taste and taste some more. Experience is ultimately the best teacher.

A New Tasting Form

To help you summarize your tasting experiences, I have developed the form which you'll find on the opposite page. The top of the form gives you spaces to record the name of the wine, along with its vintage, its country and region of origin, its price and its bottler. There is also a space to record the date of your tasting (remember, wines change with age) and your impressions of the wine's appearance.

The main body of the form is devoted to describing the wine, as perceived by your eyes, nose and mouth. What makes this form different from most others is that it's divided into two similar columns: the column on the left side of the page is devoted to the wine alone, while the one on the right is meant to describe the wine with food. In each column, there is space to record the situation surrounding the tasting, as well as the aroma and taste of the wine. This will not only enable you to remember your impressions of the wines you taste, but also make apparent how different foods affect certain parameters of the wine.

Keeping track of the situation surrounding a tasting is important. Was it a formal tasting? What other wines were present, and in what order? Or did you open it by itself, with dinner? If so, what food was present? All these factors influence the perceptions of both your nose and palate.

The section on nose allows you to quickly note how aromatic the wine is, by placing an X somewhere along the line between "light" and "powerful." Then, because impressions of aroma are always personal, there is a line to record your own thoughts. Remember, tasting is very personal. A wine can remind you of anything from ripe raspberries to hot tennis shoes.

The next section deals with the wine as perceived by your mouth: how it tastes and how it feels. There are five aspects to consider: sweetness, body, mouthfeel, acidity and finish.

NAME OF WINE _____ YEAR _____

COUNTRY _____ REGION _____ PRICE _____

BOTTLER _____ DATE TASTED _____

APPEARANCE_____

THE WINE ALONE	THE WINE WITH FOOD

SITUATION:

FOOD ACCOMPANYING WINE:

NOSE:

Light _____ Powerful

Description _____

NOSE:

Light _____ Powerful

Description _____

MOUTH:

Very sweet _____ Very dry

Light body _____ Full body

Astringent _____ Velvety

Too acid _____ Flabby

Short finish _____ Long finish

Comments: _____

MOUTH:

Very sweet _____ Very dry

Light body _____ Full body

Astringent _____ Velvety

Too acid _____ Flabby

Short finish _____ Long finish

Comments: _____

The sweetness scale refers to how much residual sugar is present in the wine. This is partly a function of how much sugar the grape contained, which in turn depends on the nature of the grape, the climate in which it was grown, and when it was harvested. The fermentation process is also an important factor, because it is at this time that a winemaker determines how much of the grape sugar is converted to alcohol and how much is allowed to remain unconverted. Wines with no residual sugar are called dry. They may taste fruity, but they are not sweet. An example is Muscadet. At the other extreme lie all those wines that are extremely sweet and almost concentrated in their taste, such as Sauternes.

Next comes body. This refers to the fullness of the wine in the mouth. A light-bodied wine seems delicate and almost dilute. This may be a positive or negative attribute, depending on the wine and what it's supposed to be. On the other hand, a wine may be full-bodied, in which case its flavour is heavy and weighty, filling the mouth completely.

Wines give the mouth not just a taste, but a feeling. Some wines are extremely harsh in the mouth, giving your tongue and cheeks a dry, furry sensation. I repeat, this is a feeling, not a taste. It is noticed mostly in young red wines which contain high levels of tannins. How astringent a wine is depends on the grape type and the method of ageing. Wines producing this furry feeling are called astringent. Wines without this property are completely different: they have a smoother texture and can be quite plush and velvety.

Acidity refers to the tartness or crispness of a wine, a characteristic important in determining how refreshing and/or how well balanced it is. In a well made, mature wine there is a good balance between fruitiness and acidity. With too much acid, the tart, sour taste predominates and all you get is pucker power. With too little acid, the wine tastes flabby; a little like flat gingerale. The wine you taste may be anywhere in between these two extremes, but hopefully not at either one.

Finally there is the finish. This refers to the impression left in your mouth by the wine after you swallow it. Does the taste linger, enabling you to still taste the wine even though you've swallowed it? If so, you say that the wine has a long finish. If its taste disappears right after swallowing, then the wine is said to have a short finish.

For each of the above characteristics, there is a line with the word describing the opposite extremes at both ends. By placing an X at the appropriate place on each line, you have a quick and easy to recall reference for that wine.

Finally, some space is left to record your thoughts about the wine. Is it over the hill? Is the high acidity a reflection of youth? Do you wish to keep it another few years before tasting again? Will it improve? Does it show good varietal or regional character? What taste memories does it bring back? What food, if any, would you like to try it with next time? These and other questions might be worth recording. Try it!

Wines Change with Time

When thinking about the characteristics of wines, it is important to remember that the fruitiness and acidity, as well as the astringency, change with time. Each of these aspects evolve and fluctuate as a wine ages.

Red wines like Barolo, Cabernet Sauvignon and Rioja tend to be long lived, with many taking ten years or more to reach their peak. In their youth, astringency and acidity dominate and mask the fruitiness. Many Bordeaux are almost undrinkable at this stage. Thankfully, the tannins precipitate out with time, and the fruit becomes more apparent. In addition, the acidity drops somewhat, with the oxidation of acids to aromatic esters. When mature, these wines exhibit a long fruit flavour, with good complexity and a pleasant balance between fruit, acidity and tannins. With time, however, even the best wines "dry out" as the fruitiness drops and the volatile acidity becomes noticeable.

Other red wines, such as many Pinot Noirs and Merlots, go through a similar life cycle. The time span is shorter, however. Tannins begin to precipitate out quickly, so that in two to three years the wine's fruitiness is showing through nicely. Unfortunately the fruit drops out almost as fast as the tannins and the wine remains at its peak for only a short time before it is "over the hill."

Light red wines, such as Beaujolais, are marked by a characteristic purply colour and high acidity when young. Unlike other red wines, they lack tannins, and so their acidity is more noticeable than their astringency. They taste fresh and fruity when young, and are best drunk this way, because the fruit declines quickly, leaving only acidity behind.

White wines are rather different from reds. Partly because of the grapes and partly because of the vinification techniques, even the best white wines start life with a fairly low level of tannins, and a relatively high amount of acidity and fruit. The amount of tannin varies, of course, with the winemaking and ageing techniques used in the production of the wine. But generally, the fruit, and especially the acidity, dominate when the wine is young. After a year or two, though, the acids are oxidized, forming aromatic esters, which enhance the perception of fruit. At maturity, there is a good balance between fruit and acid. Following this, the fruit drops and the wine loses its character. How quickly this whole process occurs depends on the quality and origin of the wine.

Body and Sweetness

Body and sweetness vary less over time than fruit and acidity. Although the wine of any region or any grape type can exhibit somewhat different styles depending on the producer and the year, there is, nonetheless, a certain typical character to most wines. Knowing how different wines rate with regard to body and sweetness could help tremendously in selecting a wine for a particular food. For example, if the concept of relativity tells you that you need a dry, full-bodied red wine for your dinner, you need some way of finding out which red wines are indeed full-bodied and dry. Likewise for light wines, sweet wines, white wines and so on.

The next pages depict these dimensions of sweetness and body in a graphic manner. Notice that there is one graph for white wines and another for red. On each graph, the vertical axis represents dryness, going from very dry at the bottom to very sweet at the top. The horizontal axis depicts body, with the most light-bodied on the left to the most full-bodied on the right. Every wine on the graph is placed in its relative position with regard to each of these dimensions, remembering, of course, that any type of wine will differ somewhat from producer to producer and from year to year. The chart is meant, not as gospel, but as a fencepost, something on which to hang your hat, and as a guide in selecting wines for different occasions.

Suppose that for a particular dish you are looking for a white wine that is very dry and light. The driest and lightest are listed in the bottom left corner of the chart. Your personal preference and budget will help you make a selection from this group. If you have seen a wine that intrigues you but having never tasted it you have no idea of what it's like, it's position on the chart will help you to determine its nature. At this point you can be assured of making an intelligent decision about whether to buy it or not. (Buying a wine you have never tasted before, and discovering all its hidden secrets, will never lose its intrigue, even with a chart!)

WINE SELECTION GUIDE

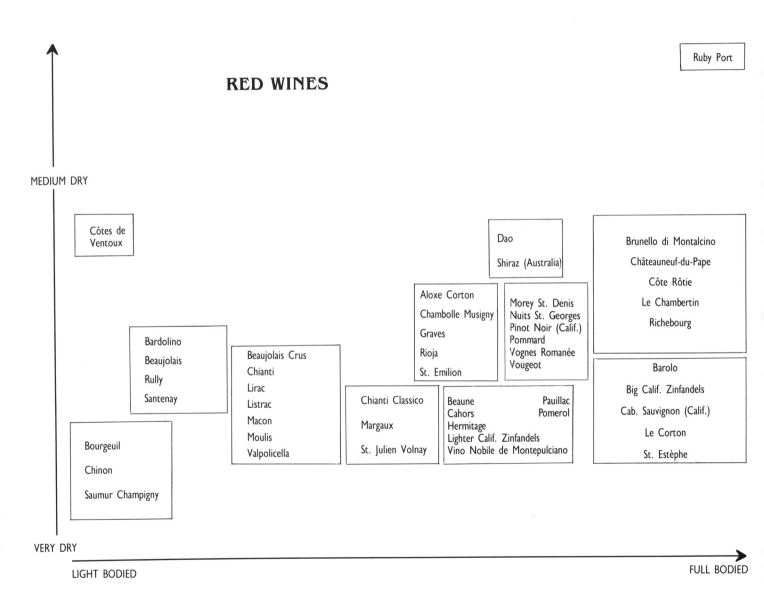

RED WINES

Ruby Port

MEDIUM DRY

Côtes de Ventoux

Dao
Shiraz (Australia)

Brunello di Montalcino
Châteauneuf-du-Pape
Côte Rôtie
Le Chambertin
Richebourg

Aloxe Corton
Chambolle Musigny
Graves
Rioja
St. Emilion

Morey St. Denis
Nuits St. Georges
Pinot Noir (Calif.)
Pommard
Vognes Romanée
Vougeot

Bardolino
Beaujolais
Rully
Santenay

Beaujolais Crus
Chianti
Lirac
Listrac
Macon
Moulis
Valpolicella

Barolo
Big Calif. Zinfandels
Cab. Sauvignon (Calif.)
Le Corton
St. Estèphe

Chianti Classico
Margaux
St. Julien Volnay

Beaune   Pauillac
Cahors   Pomerol
Hermitage
Lighter Calif. Zinfandels
Vino Nobile de Montepulciano

Bourgeuil
Chinon
Saumur Champigny

VERY DRY

LIGHT BODIED

FULL BODIED

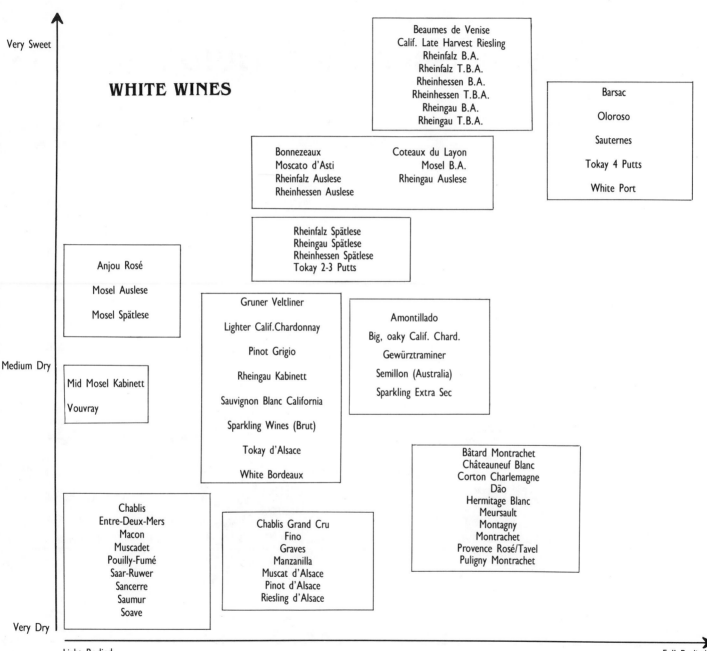

WHITE WINES

Very Sweet

Beaumes de Venise
Calif. Late Harvest Riesling
Rheinfalz B.A.
Rheinfalz T.B.A.
Rheinhessen B.A.
Rheinhessen T.B.A.
Rheingau B.A.
Rheingau T.B.A.

Barsac

Oloroso

Sauternes

Tokay 4 Putts

White Port

Bonnezeaux
Moscato d'Asti
Rheinfalz Auslese
Rheinhessen Auslese

Coteaux du Layon
Mosel B.A.
Rheingau Auslese

Rheinfalz Spätlese
Rheingau Spätlese
Rheinhessen Spätlese
Tokay 2-3 Putts

Anjou Rosé

Mosel Auslese

Mosel Spätlese

Gruner Veltliner

Lighter Calif. Chardonnay

Pinot Grigio

Rheingau Kabinett

Sauvignon Blanc California

Sparkling Wines (Brut)

Tokay d'Alsace

White Bordeaux

Amontillado

Big, oaky Calif. Chard.

Gewürztraminer

Semillon (Australia)

Sparkling Extra Sec

Medium Dry

Mid Mosel Kabinett

Vouvray

Bâtard Montrachet
Châteauneuf Blanc
Corton Charlemagne
Dão
Hermitage Blanc
Meursault
Montagny
Montrachet
Provence Rosé/Tavel
Puligny Montrachet

Chablis
Entre-Deux-Mers
Macon
Muscadet
Pouilly-Fumé
Saar-Ruwer
Sancerre
Saumur
Soave

Chablis Grand Cru
Fino
Graves
Manzanilla
Muscat d'Alsace
Pinot d'Alsace
Riesling d'Alsace

Very Dry

Light Bodied

Full Bodied

A Guide to Grapes

In order to make more sophisticated choices, some knowledge of grape types is needed. Grapes, after all, are the main ingredient of any wine. In spite of the magical transformation that occurs during fermentation and ageing, it is still the taste of the grape that is a major determinant in the taste of any wine. If you ever travel to wine country during harvest time, this is very apparent. Different grapes look and taste different! I remember tasting Riesling grapes in Germany one autumn. Lo and behold, the grapes were highly acidic, and had that same ''Riesling character'' I had learned to identify in the wines! Amazing when experienced for the first time, but perfectly logical. A wine's basic character is a result of the grape from which it is made.

Understanding the grapes that go into wine therefore gives you a tremendous advantage both in selecting wines and in matching food and wine. Even if you have never seen a particular wine before, as long as you know (or find out) its main grape type, you are off to the races. You can predict with a fair amount of accuracy what it will taste like, and therefore what you might want to pair it with. Let's take a look, then, at some of the world's major grapes.

Cabernet Sauvignon

The Cabernet Sauvignon vine is said to have originated in Bordeaux. Today it is the principle grape in most Médoc wines, contributing to a lesser but varying degree to the (red) wines of Graves and St. Emilion. The red wines of Anjou and Saumur also use some Cabernet Sauvignon. However this vine does not limit itself to France. It has been successfully transplanted to Australia, New Zealand, South Africa, Chile, Argentina and California.

Cabernet Sauvignon produces a highly tannic, and astringent wine. This is because the grapes have thick black skins that contain a concentration of tannic acids. Furthermore the grapes are small, so that there is a tremendous amount of skin area for the amount of pulp and juice. Because the skin of Cabernet

Sauvignon grapes is heavily pigmented, the wine it produces tends to have a deep colour.

Both the tannin and the acidity of Cabernet Sauvignon wines will vary, however, with the soil and microclimate in which the vine was grown, the age of the wine, as well as with the methods used in vinification and ageing.

The vine grows best on stony ground, where its roots have easy access to deep underground water. This is because its roots are the type that penetrate deeply into the earth as opposed to spreading out just beneath the surface.

Cabernet Sauvignon wines are long lived, sometimes requiring 10 to 20 or more years to reach their peak. When young they often exude a herbaceous, leathery aroma. As they mature the aroma changes to become incredibly complex, often reminiscent of blackcurrants and cedar. Depending on the wine, its origin and its age, you might also detect the aroma of violets, lead pencil, freshly tarred pavement, or cigar box.

In the mouth a good Cabernet Sauvignon is big, chewy and full-bodied, with complex flavour patterns and an interesting balance between fruit and oak. It makes a perfect partner for strongly flavoured meats like lamb and game, as well as beef. Although harsh when young, Cabernet Sauvignons soften with age to produce one of the world's truly great wines.

Pinot Noir

Pinot Noir is the vine that has given Burgundy its reputation for great red wines. The heartland for the Pinot Noir is, in fact, Burgundy's Côte d'Or where according to Michael Broadbent, it produces wines ''of sublime richness and quality.'' Over time, the vine has spread northward into Champagne, especially around the mountain of Reims, and southward into the Maconnais. It is planted in California as well, although it has not become one of the area's strong points. This is because the Pinot Noir needs cooler weather, small temperature fluctuations, calciferous soils and a greater availability of water from rainfall (that is, surface water) rather than from deep root sources.

The Pinot Noir grapes grow in very compact bunches that look remarkably like large pine cones. It is this pine cone shape that has given its name (from the French word 'pin') to the Pinot.

The grapes themselves are blue-black in colour. They yield a large amount of colourless juice that tends to be quite sweet in good years and highly acidic. Because of the relatively large proportion of juice in relation to skin, Pinot Noir wines are less tannic but more acidic than Cabernet Sauvignon.

A good Pinot Noir should have an aroma which is sweeter and less austere than a Cabernet Sauvignon, tending more toward ripe red fruit in nature. However there is more to the Pinot nose than fruit. It is absolutely unique, very recognizable but very difficult to put into words. Well known wine professional Michael Broadbent calls it "boiled beetroot." David Hanson, in his authoritative book on Burgundy, refers to it as "not straightforwardly grapy, or plummy, or floral; it is as if the odour of a recently shot game bird mingled with that of the leaf-mould on which it fell. The result is neither animal nor vegetable, but both appetizing and intriguing."

The colour and body of a Pinot Noir will vary according to its origin – ranging from a rich ruby colour to a lighter hue; and from medium to full-bodied. It is soft and velvety in texture, and possesses a good balance between acidity and fruit. The right food for this wine depends on its origin and style. In general, beef dishes bring out the best in a Pinot.

Merlot

Merlot is a widely grown grape thriving best on clay soil. It is found in the Pomerol and St. Emilion regions of France, and in Italy, North America, South America and Africa. Although the Italians and Californians often produce Merlot varietals, the French usually blend the grape with others. The amount used in any blend depends on the region and the château. For example, in the Médoc, Merlot contributes 40 per cent or less to most blends, while in Pomerol, it can make up as much as 90 per cent.

The grapes are small, with thin skins and therefore tend to produce round, soft wines, low in tannins. These characteristics, along with the plummy fruitiness, make Merlot an excellent blending grape, that helps to add soft fruit and a certain roundness to wines that would otherwise be tannic and austere. Wines with a high concentration of Merlot often go well with pheasant, rabbit or pork dishes, as well as with beef.

Gamay Noir à Jus Blanc

Gamay Noir (à Jus Blanc) takes its name from a small hamlet of the same name, situated very close to the classic village of Puligny-Montrachet in the Côte d'Or, where, interestingly enough, no Gamay grows today.

Gamay Noir is used in the making of Beaujolais, and also in many of the wines from Mâcon. In other parts of Burgundy it is part of Bourgogne Passe-Tous-Grains (along with Pinot Noir). The vine has not been transplanted as successfully on other continents as, let's say, the Cabernet Sauvignon. Gamay Beaujolais, as grown in California and Canada, is not a member of the Gamay family.

Although the Gamay vine will grow well on limestone, or on clay-limestone, it is at its best in the Beaujolais region, where the soil is composed of degenerating sandstone or granite.

The Gamay Noir is not usually grown in hedgerows, as are most other vines. It is pruned in the shape of a goblet in order that the fruit will be held on the inside of the plant, shielded from direct sunlight. In this way, growers are able to retain a very high fresh and fruity acidity in the grapes.

The Gamay vine is a more fruitful plant than Cabernet Sauvignon or Sauvignon Blanc, producing small bunches composed of medium-sized, oval berries which yield a clear juice. From it is produced a rather flippant wine that is light, fresh and fruity, with lots of acidity, but little tannin, and hence at its best when drunk young. Slightly chilled, Gamay makes a perfect summer picnic wine. It also goes well with many pastas, cheeses and lighter meat dishes.

Syrah

The Syrah vine is grown in the northern Rhône, on extremely arid slopes and terraces in what is essentially a sun-drenched valley. Originally, this vine was brought by Phoenician traders from Syria, hence its name.

It is a particularly low yielding variety, producing very dark and rather sweet grapes. The Syrah vine is not planted much outside France, although it does appear in California, in South Africa and in Australia, where it is known as Shiraz.

Its wines are inclined to be deep in colour and tannic when very young. Because of the high sugar content of Syrah grapes, the wines tend to be high in alcohol. The aroma of Syrah wines is reminiscent of cherries and redcurrants, often with floral or spicy attributes. In the mouth, they are usually full-bodied, with tannic fruitiness. They should make a beautiful complement to strongly flavoured meat dishes.

Grenache

Grenache is also grown in the Rhône producing, along with other varieties, the great wines of Châteauneuf-du-Pape. It is a grape which absolutely adores the very hot climate of the southern Rhône.

Because of the climate in which it grows, Grenache is a sweet grape. It therefore produces a wine that is high in alcohol. That alcohol has a distinct effect in the production of bouquet, often described as being similar to pimentos or green peppers.

Grenache is known as Garnacha in Spain, where it contributes to the making of Rioja wines. In southern France, it is also known as the Alicante, often going into the production of very cheap table wines. Only in Châteauneuf-du-Pape does it produce wines of outstanding quality, showing strength and body ideally suited to accompany red meats. Châteauneuf-du-Pape has relatively low tannin and acidity and should be drunk within ten years of bottling.

Zinfandel

Although Zinfandel is now unique to California, its origins are controversial. Recent research at the Univeristy of California has shown that its closest relative may be an Italian grape variety, possibly brought to the U.S. in 1851 by Agoston Haraszthy.

Zinfandel's bluish, violet-coloured grapes grow best on hillsides having a soil that is slightly sandy, with a definite limestone component – as for instance, the high hillsides of the Napa Valley. The wines made from Zinfandel often show great depth of colour, with a bouquet reminiscent of spicy raspberries.

Although there are many different styles of Zinfandel, the present trend is toward a soft, fruity wine with medium body. However Zinfandel can be deep and powerful (as in Ridge), elegant (as in Simi or Clos du Val) and can possess varying amounts of complexity, depending on its vinification and origin.

Late Harvest Zinfandel is produced by leaving the grapes on the vines longer into the autumn in order to increase their sugar content. The resulting wine is sweet, rich and powerful, with as much as 20 per cent alcohol. Its taste is so intense that some experts say it is the perfect match for chocolate desserts!

Chardonnay

Although Chardonnay has been in Burgundy for many centuries, it is thought that the wine originated in the area of Limersol in southern Cypress and was brought back to France by returning crusaders.

Chardonnay is the vine used for the great white wines of the Côte d'Or – wines such as Le Montrachet, Meursault, and Corton Charlemagne. A little further north in Chablis, it is the only vine permitted. Here it is known as the Beaunois. The vine has also spread south to the Mâconnais, where it makes such wines as Pouilly-Vinzelles and Saint Véran. It has now been transplanted with great success to the southern hemisphere and to California, where it is as successful – perhaps because of marketing as much as quality – as any other variety.

Its berries are small, but very rich in white juice which is delicately sugared.

Chardonnay normally produces a wine that is 12 to 12½ per cent alcohol, pale straw to straw yellow in colour, with an aroma that is crisp and fruity, sometimes with overtones of oak, or flintiness or a buttery nuttiness. In the mouth, Chardonnays can range from light and crisp, as in the case of many Chablis, to quite full-bodied, as in the case of many Meursaults, or of course, Le Montrachet. Here again, the style of a Chardonnay can vary, depending on the climate and soil it comes from, as well as its vinification and ageing. Along with the basic fruitiness can be found a low or high acidity, a subtle or not-so-subtle oakiness, sometimes a certain flintiness. It may be prefaced by a buttery, nutty nose. These complexities make Chardonnay a facinating wine and a perfect companion for many different fish and seafood dishes.

Riesling

Riesling is also known as Johannisberg Riesling, Rhine Riesling and True Riesling. Rhine Riesling is probably the most correct, since its original site of development was indeed in the Rhine Valley, probably in the Rheingau.

The true (Rhine) Riesling has spread along the river basin of the Rhine itself and now encompasses plantings in the Mosel, all the way down the Rhine and into Switzerland. From there, it has spread into Austria and then down the Danube Valley toward the Black Sea. In Alsace, the Riesling is also very successful, producing a dry, crisp wine that is very aromatic and very elegant.

However, Riesling is a vine with certain difficulties. Firstly, it flowers fairly late, and bears fruit relatively late. If not assured a good climate with the proper amount of sun and rain during the summer, it does not mature by the time the often inclement weather comes in the autumn. On the other hand it is well suited to late harvest wines and the delight of botrytis cinerea.

The Riesling vine grows particularly well in rocky, slaty soils such as those found in the Mosel and in the Rheingau. In recent years, it has been transplanted to California, where it is known as the Johannisberg Riesling, and to Canada, where some growers are having remarkable success.

Riesling produces a very delicately perfumed wine which some experts say has the aroma of lychees or other oriental fruits. Others liken it to orange blossoms or other flowers; some simply call it fruity and fresh, as indeed it is in the mouth. At times, Riesling is steely or honeyed and sweet. In fact, Riesling exhibits many different faces, depending on its origin and its vinification. It can be flowery, steely or fruity, it can be soft or austere; and it can range from very dry to intensely sweet. Yet there is a basic Riesling character – the grape itself – that ties together all these dimensions.

Because of this versatility, Riesling can be enjoyed in a variety of situations. The Germans drink semi-dry Riesling with everything, claiming that it provides a refreshing counterpoint to any food, no matter how heavy. Indeed, I have enjoyed it with many different foods – from appetizers through to desserts, of course saving the sweetest (and best) to the last!

Sauvignon Blanc

Sauvignon Blanc is known as the white grape of Bordeaux, although it has been transplanted extensively to many parts of the world.

Sauvignon Blanc produces "fumé" wines. They are not smoky, as the name suggests; rather they have the flavour of gooseberries. The vine is an astringent and pungent plant with a concentrated perfume.

In France, it is found near the headwaters of the Loire, in Bordeaux and also in Tourraine. In Sancerre and Pouilly-sur-Loire, the grape is extremely successful, as indeed it can be in Bordeaux. Until recently, the Sauvignon Blanc played a supporting role in Bordeaux, being blended with the sweeter, more full-bodied Semillon. In recent years, however, some communes are producing wines with a predominance of Sauvignon Blanc, in order to follow the trend for dry, light wines.

Sauvignon Blanc is even more of a shy bearer than Cabernet Sauvignon. This is actually encouraged. If the vine is allowed to develop too prolifically, the resulting wines lose their fresh, attractive acidity. Sauvignon Blanc produces dry white wines with a distinctly grassy aroma, although many British people liken it to gooseberries (a fruit I must admit I've never seen much less smelled!). In Bordeaux, when blended with Semillon, the resulting wine exhibits good body and depth of character. Some areas, Entre-Deux-Mers, or Sancerre, for example, produce lighter, drier wines with good acidity, making them well suited either to delicate fish dishes or to cheeses like chèvre which have a high acidity and need a high acid wine to match.

Gewürztraminer

Gewürztraminer means "spicy traminer," which is intended to be a reflection of the rather strong and complex aroma of the wine, not an implication of spiciness.

The Gewürztraminer vine is at its best in Alsace and Germany, especially in the Rheinpfalz, although it has also been transplanted to California, northeastern Italy, Yugoslavia and Switzerland.

The ripening period of Gewürztraminer is shorter than that of the Riesling. The unfermented juice of Gewürztraminer has a strong perfume rather like peaches and apricots, with a hint of herbs. Sometimes an aroma of lychees is evident. The juice itself has quite a strong colour, which comes from the pinky skins of the ripe grapes.

Once fermented, the juice becomes pale to medium yellow. It can be dry (as in Alsace) or semi-dry (as in Germany). In either case it is distinctive and assertive – a wine that can stand up well to strongly flavoured foods such as smoked cheese or smoked fish.

WINE AND CHEESE

No book on wine is complete without discussing wine and cheese. The two have been enjoyed together as long as anyone can remember. Why and how the team first paired up is somewhat obscure, but now their relationship is so taken for granted that no one really questions it.

What really makes them go together so well? It's time to take a closer look and examine how the principles discussed in the last chapter apply to this "dynamic duo."

Millions of people have been enjoying wine and cheese for years and years, both in North America and in Europe. In France especially, it is common to see a cheese plate after the main course, supposedly to help finish off the wine in your glass. In North America, the popularity of wine and cheese parties would not have become such an institution were there not some degree of pleasure attached to the combination. So there must exist a certain level of at least casual enjoyment from wine and cheese.

However, two groups of people dispute this. First are the serious wine tasters and second the serious cheese tasters. Both these groups claim the same thing; that wine and cheese detract from each other. The wine people of course, argue that cheese masks or changes the flavour of the wine. The cheese people, as expected, claim that the wine prevents you from really appreciating the flavour of the cheese.

This leaves us in an awkward position. Do we believe the connoisseurs? If so, what happens to all our pleasant wine and cheese memories? The Sauternes that was gorgeous together with the Roquefort and how enjoyable it was to finish that 1970 Château Figeac with a piece of Cheddar. Should these be erased from your memory and all future invitations to wine and cheese parties be refused? What is the "right" thing to say next time the topic of wine and cheese comes up in a conversation?

The right answer really lies in your situation or purpose. If you are involved in serious wine tasting or commercial purchasing, beware of cheese: it will alter your perceptions of the wines you taste, usually in the direction of masking defects. Bread would be a more appropriate mouth cleanser. If you are doing any serious cheese tasting, beware of drinking too much wine, as alcohol can affect your ability to think clearly, and besides, it will alter your perceptions of the cheese. However, if you are out for general enjoyment, then the very reason that makes wine and cheese inappropriate for those ''serious'' tasters – namely the tendency of wine and cheese to hide each other's faults – now makes it totally appropriate. In other words, if you're out for simple pleasure (and what's wrong with that?) why not take advantage of this taste altering and make it work for you? But make sure you know how...

The basis for understanding wine and cheese interactions lies in kitchen chemistry where the concept of counterbalance plays the important role. A characteristic of one item, perhaps unpleasant alone, can be counteracted or counterbalanced by an equal and opposite characteristic of another item. Counterbalance acts like Newton's law in physics that every action has an equal and opposite reaction.

In the case of wine and cheese, the acidity of the wine is counterbalanced by the alkalinity of the cheese. There are also contrasts in texture and mouthfeel. The cheese is often pasty or mouthcoating, for instance, while many wines are crisp and cleansing or astringent due to the presence of tannins. The more mouthcoating a cheese, therefore, the more the wine needs acidity or astringency, to cut through. However this does not mean that all cheese goes with all wine.

Relative strengths of both aroma and flavour should be the same for both the cheese and the wine. That is, robust wine should go with strongly flavoured cheese and lighter wine with milder cheese. Think carefully about aroma; if the cheese and the wine are both highly aromatic, do you really want to be faced with two scents at once? Decide. Will the scent of the cheese fight with and detract from your appreciation of the wine's bouquet? Which do you want to place on center stage? Can they really share the spotlight?

Remember, too, that cheese changes with time. Like wine, cheese undergoes an ageing process. During that process, its characteristics will change somewhat. Cheddar is one familiar example. The strength of its flavour increases dramatically as it ages. In some cheeses, the perception of acidity, or sourness, also increases with the age of the cheese. If so, the acidity of the wine must be correspondingly high so that it matches that of the cheese. If it does not match, the cheese will make the wine appear flat and flabby.

The type of milk used in the production of a cheese has a major influence on the taste of the final product. Although most cheeses today are made from cow's milk, there are many made from the milk of ewes and goats. These are richer in protein and fat than cow's milk and hence produce different (often richer) types of cheese.

Even the milk (and hence the cheese) of a single animal can vary in taste depending on the breed of the animal, the particular vegetation upon which the animal grazed (there is a transference of flavour from the mineral composition of the soil) or the treatment of the milk (e.g. raw or pasteurized).

Still more variations are produced during the ageing process. Length of ageing plays a role, as well as the type of microorganism involved. In some cases, a bacteria or mold is naturally present and in some cases it is introduced. In either event, its action produces predictable changes in both flavour and texture.

In fact, describing the taste of cheese is much like describing the taste of wine. There are innumerable variations. To keep track of hundreds of individual cheeses becomes somewhat difficult. We are much better off developing some kind of taste-oriented classification system requiring only that we learn the sensory characteristics (and wine matches!) of a dozen or so types of cheese. When faced with a new cheese, we simply determine what type it is and voilà! We instantly know something about our new "friend." With time and experience we form impressions about the differences and nuances between members of any category and refine our judgements, just as we do with wine.

A very useful classification of cheeses is outlined in the Table on page 44. With these categories in mind we can begin to think about choosing wines for the occasion when you want the two together on a "simple enjoyment" level.

Cheddar type cheeses have a very pronounced flavour that tends to stay with you due to their mouthcoating properties. There is no question that you need a full-bodied wine to hold up to these cheeses. I prefer assertive reds. However, it is important to realize that the nutty-sour flavour of Cheddar type cheeses fights somewhat with young, grapy, berryish reds. Cheddars harmonize much better with well-aged, complex wines having an oaky, earthy aspect, or the kind of cedar and tobacco components you get in older Bordeaux. The sharper the cheddar, the more the wine needs acidity and character.

Dutch cheeses are easy to eat and can be matched to a variety of wines. Their flavour is neither light nor heavy. The intensity of a red wine should therefore match. Light to medium-bodied reds, like many Merlots, would go well. Because of the smooth buttery texture of these cheeses, they also marry well with light refreshing whites. Those with some sweetness, or a distinct fruitiness, contrast nicely.

When serving Italian cheeses, do as the natives do, and drink Italian wine.

Cheese Classifications

TYPE	CHARACTERISTICS	EXAMPLES
Cheddar	mild to sharp flavour depending on the length of age-ing; often described as nutty; some members more salty and sour; firm texture	Cheddar, Colby, Derby, Cheshire
Dutch	flavour varies in intensity; most are light and buttery, slightly nutty; smooth texture	Gouda, Edam, Tilsit
Stringlike Italian	Italian cheeses, used mostly in cooking; can range from mild to salty and piquant	Mozzarella, Provolone, Caciocavallo
Swiss	semi-firm to firm texture, having small or large holes; sweetish, nutty taste	Emmentaler, Gruyère, Samsoe, Jarlsberg, Fontina
Blue	blue-green streaks arise from the injection of mould, giving the cheese its characteristically piquant flavour; many are quite high in both acid and salt; some have a very soft, creamy base and others are more crumbly	Roquefort, Gorgonzola, Stilton, Pipo Crème, Bleu d'Auvergne, Bleu de Bresse, Danish Blue
Surface Ripened	soft or semi-soft; creamy and smooth with a delicate, mellow flavour some are slightly salty, often very rich and high in fat	Brie, Camembert, Esrom
Crèmes	mostly French, very high in fat content, often 60-70%; extremely smooth, soft and rich	Double and Triple Crèmes, L'Explorateur, Boursin
Spiced	cheeses which have had spices or herbs added during processing, e.g., caraway, pepper, garlic, etc.	Spiced gouda, Boursin with garlic and herbs
Chèvres	distinct 'goaty' taste, often quite sour; vary from soft to firm, creamy to drier; mild aroma	Montrachet, Bucheron, Le Banon
Monastery	many originated in monasteries; smooth, semi-firm; vary in intensity of taste and aroma, a strong 'earthy' or 'mushroomy' component	Oka, Pont L'Evêque, Tomme de Savoie, Havarti, Muenster

Taken from *Completely Cheese*, Jonathan David, publisher. By Anita May Pearl and co-workers.

Whether to serve white or red, and then which one, depends on the particular cheese and what it's covering. Provolone especially can be quite mild or very piquant. Remember always to match intensities. Frankly, I avoid using too much of a very strong cheese. There is no point in having one component of one dish dominate everything else in the meal. You're better off with a tease because it does a much better job at exciting both the palate and the mind, leaving room for enjoyment of both food and wine. A fruity, well-structured red is usually a good partner to the medium weight cheese in this group – like eating cheese and fruit – but in this case you are drinking the fruit rather than eating it. However, if the cheese is very mild, like mozzarella, and the accompanying food is also mild, then a light, refreshing white to refresh the palate is in order. Soave or Pinot Grigio (Friuli) are examples of wines that would do beautifully.

Swiss cheeses have a mild but distinctly nutty flavour, often with just a hint of sweetness. Although their texture is firm, the fat content of Swiss cheeses is often quite high. White wines with a crisp acidity help to liven them up, while the fat content of the cheese, in turn, helps to temper the acidity of the wine. Suitable wines include French Muscadet, Swiss Neufchâtel, or Canadian Seyval Blanc. On a different note, try a tawny port; it tends to accentuate the nuttiness of these cheeses.

Blue cheeses need to be matched with extreme care, as their assertive character tends to overpower most wines. Although they vary tremendously, many blues are salty, sour and "mouldy" (yet quite delightful) tasting. To stand up to this, a wine needs to have an acidity to match that of the cheese, and an intensity of flavour to counterbalance the "blue" taste. Two kinds of wine will do this: my first choice are the botrycized wines like Sauternes; my second choice would be the very full-bodied reds with the long finishes. In England, port and Stilton are a favourite combination.

Surface ripened cheeses like Brie and Camembert are delicate and mellow in taste. In order not to be overpowered, they need relatively delicate wines. Crisp, fruity wines like Riesling or Gamay form interesting and complementary partners.

Double and Triple Crèmes are creamy and smooth, filling the mouth with their richness. They are complemented beautifully by red wines with a definite berry type taste like Chinon, Volnay, or other elegant Burgundies. If you like heavier, but very fruity reds, then a Californian Cabernet Sauvignon or Zinfandel would do, or from Spain, the Torres Gran Coronas Black Label. In whites, an Alsatian Gewürztraminer would be interesting because of its high acidity and its aromatic nature.

Gewürztraminer really comes into its own, with smoked or spiced cheeses. With this group, the strong flavour of the smoke would carry on in the mouth and dominate delicate wines. The nice thing about Gewürztraminer is that its flavour is both assertive and complementary to a spiced cheese. Smoky cheeses similarly demand a smoky wine. Canadian Chelois or Alsatian Tokay come to mind.

Chèvres are highly acidic and distinctly "goaty." To match their acidity, a Cabernet Franc or Gamay would be suitable or in a white, a Sauvignon Blanc, such as a Sancerre.

Monastery cheeses vary in the intensity of their taste and aroma, but most have a noticeably earthy or mushroomy component. A cheese in this group demands a wine with a taste intensity to match its own. Alsatian Muscat or Gewürztraminer usually go well with Muenster and other strongly flavoured members of this group. St. Emilion and some Burgundies blend well with the milder ones, such as Havarti.

The chart which follows summarizes my wine and cheese suggestions. It is by no means exhaustive. Rather, it is a starting point for your enjoyment.

CHEESE TYPE	WINE SUGGESTIONS
Cheddar	well-aged Cabernet Sauvignon, older style Rioja. Tawny Port, dry Amarone.
Dutch	Chenin Blanc; Merlot; Riesling; some Spanish whites, Valpolicella, dry Amarone.
Italian	Pinot Grigio (Friuli), Orvieto, Soave; Italian Merlot, Chianti; Brunello di Montalcino, Barolo.
Swiss	Swiss Neufchatel, Canadian Seyval Blanc, most Alsatians, Muscadet, Tawny Port, dry Amarone.
Blue	Sauternes, Alsatian Vendange Tardif, German Beernenauslese or Trockenbeerenauslese, Port, full-bodied reds such as California Zinfandel, Italian Barolo, some French Burgundies, Australian Shiraz, Canadian Maréchal Foch.
Surface Ripened	Gamay, Riesling Spätlese or Auslese, Chenin Blanc (e.g. Vouvray).
Crèmes	Chinon, elegant Burgundies, California Zinfandel or Cabernet Sauvignon, Torres Gran Coronas Black Label, Alsatian Gewürztraminer.
Spiced	Gewürztraminer (Alsatian or German), Canadian Chelois, Tokay d'Alsace.
Chèvres	Cabernet Franc (e.g. Chinon), Gamay (e.g. Beaujolais), Sauvignon Blanc, such as Sancerre.
Monastery	Alsatian Muscat or Gewürztraminer, St. Emilion, Burgundy, dry Amarone.

PART II

A
GASTRONOMIC
TOUR

THE FOOD AND WINE
OF ALSACE

Alsace is a particularly fascinating area to study from both a sensory and an intellectual point of view. Its location at the northeast corner of France is the first key to unlocking its story. If you look at the map, you can see that Alsace is a long finger of land, flanked on one side by the Voges mountains, on the other by the Rhine river (and not far into Germany by the Black Forest mountains). This gives the region a continental climate with fairly hot summers and cold harsh winters.

The vineyards of Alsace are located on the eastern slopes of the Voges, with the winds and the weather coming from the west. Rain is thus prevalent on the western side of the range, with the eastern (Alsatian) side being noticeably drier and sunnier – especially in the summer. This protective effect is most noticeable in the more southern (Haut-Rhin) area of Alsace, where the mountains are highest. The net result is that the grapes develop a concentration of flavour and fragrance not found in wetter regions. Yet the sun and the dryness are accompanied by temperatures low enough to permit the grapes to retain a high degree of acidity that results in the clean refreshing aspect so characteristic of Alsatian wines. The soil varies greatly along the entire length of the region, as do specific microclimates. This has permitted Alsatians to grow a number of different grape types with remarkable success.

Gewürztraminer is one of the varietals for which Alsace is famous. The word "gewürz," in German, means "spice" and spice is generally what Gewürztraminer is all about. The wine on its own is sometimes too strong, but that same forcefulness is what makes it such an ideal accompaniment to many Alsatian specialties.

Riesling is considered by Alsatians as the king of wines. From the grape of the same name, the Riesling wine of Alsace is less forward than the Gewürztraminers, less full-bodied than the Tokays – yet it towers over both of these in its elegance and finesse. The Riesling grape grows well on the chalky soil near Ribeauville and Riquewihr, producing a dry fruity wine with high acidity and good varietal character.

Tokay of Alsace bears no resemblance to the sweet Hungarian wines of the same name. Coming from the Pinot Gris grape, the Tokay d'Alsace is often described as opulent, lush and full of body; fruity with a hint of smokiness, sometimes slightly honeyed. It is a traditional accompaniment to foie gras.

Most wines made from the *Muscat* grape are sweet and grapy. By contrast, in Alsace, the Muscat wine retains its characteristic grapyness, yet is vinified dry. The result is a surprisingly clean and refreshing wine. As a result, Alsatians often drink this wine as an apéritif, or at the end of a meal with some locally made Muenster cheese.

The focus on varietal and the position of Riesling in the order of things is more reminiscent of Germany than of France. At first, this might seem curious. Yet a glimpse through history reminds us quickly that Alsace was not always a French province. Between 1870 and 1914 and then between 1940 and 1944, it fell under German control. Germany made its presence felt in Alsace, in everything from architecture to dress customs and, of course, in eating and drinking.

The influence of Germany on Alsatian winemaking is best described by winemaker Jean Hugel in his remark that ''Alsace makes Germanic wine in the French way.'' In other words, they start with some of the same grape varieties, for example, Riesling, but they vinify it differently. The Germans aim for sweetness, stressing the need for balance between sugar and acid. The Alsatians aim for strength of flavour, preferring a dry, clean wine with lots of acidity and no residual sugar. Alsatian wines are well suited to accompany the area's creamy, rich food.

The food of Alsace, like its wines, is a reflection of its mixed heritage. As in Germany, the pig and the goose play important roles in furnishing both meat and fat – both meant to be filling and sustaining. Yet the end result is not identical. Having a French background too, the Alsatians have managed to muster up just enough subtlety and imagination to give a French touch to a German recipe. For instance, only in Alsace would they take the lowly goose of Germany and get from it the delicacy called foie gras.

Geese have been plentiful in Alsace, as in Germany, for hundreds of years. They are omnivorous creatures and inexpensive to keep. The Alsatians of German heritage were accustomed to raising them. But before that, the Romans showed a considerable interest in geese. The liver of the goose was especially liked, even considered a delicacy. The Romans made a practice of soaking the extracted liver in milk to make it richer and heavier. In more recent times, the liver has been fattened by force-feeding the goose. This somewhat objectionable technique involves feeding the geese beyond their wishes, often through a funnel inserted into the throat! A gruesome practice perhaps, but it yields incredible results.

In the eighteenth century, a Norman cook by the name of Close had the idea of using a goose liver (fattened or not, is rather hard to say) to make a pâté. He added truffles for flavour and enclosed the pâté in a golden pastry. For a long time, this dish was reserved exclusively for the Maréchal de Contades, the commander of the province. Then, near the end of the eighteenth century, the Maréchal left Alsace and Close began to sell his specialty to the public, making it more widely accessible than ever before. Perhaps that is why Close is often accredited with the invention of foie gras in general. Actually it is important to remember that Close did not invent the foie gras itself for that merely depends on how the goose was fed! What Close did do, is introduce a pâté, made from foie gras.

Close's recipe for pâté de foie gras was modified in later years by a Bordeaux born chef named Doyon, who had settled in Strasbourg. Doyon's restaurant still exists.

My own first experience with pâté de foie gras came while I was visiting a well noted inn in Alsace, the Château d'Isenbourg. It was presented in a most elegant way, with the slice of pale pink pâté occupying centre stage on a white plate, garnished simply by a small leaf of lettuce topped with a tomato rose. The pâté was incredible. I'm not sure what I enjoyed more, its taste or its texture. Both were fantastically rich. Smooth in the mouth, it felt like a combination of velvet and silk. The taste was amazingly mild and sweet with just a hint of "liver" taste. It was complemented perfectly by a glass of Tokay: opulant and full-bodied, with a hint of honey and a suggestion of smoke, enough weight to match the pâté, yet enough acidity to clean and refresh the palate. All in all, the kind of deliciousness that makes you want to order another round of both food and wine (but you don't because you're too embarrassed!) In any case, dishes like pâté de foie gras definitely rank with foods for the gods, or at least, the nobility!

Choucroute is a completely different story. Often said to be the national dish of Alsace, its history goes back a long way. Fifteenth century records describe cabbage being shredded, then salted and stored in barrels with an assortment of seasonings, including dill, horseradish, cumin and elderberry leaves. Today, bay leaves, cloves and juniper berries are added to the cabbage during its three weeks or so of pickling.

It is then prepared in the following way by food writer, Waverly Root:

"It is cooked in a pan whose bottom has been lined with pork fat, along with a few onions, each with a clove inserted in it, cut up carrots, a bunch of herbs, and juniper berries. What goes in then may depend considerably on the fantasy of the cook. If it is à la Strasbourgeoise it is probably a hunk of pork from the breast of the animal, another piece of smoked pork, and lard, or, better, goose grease. This is covered with consommé, strips of fat pork are placed on top, and it is cooked slowly in a closed dish for about four hours, the pork being taken out after the first hour, to be restored only when the dish is served..."

In the past, choucroute was served with boiled root vegetables and "lard fumé." On special occasions sausages were added, or sometimes goose. Today if you order choucroute in Alsace you are liable to be presented with a mound of the choucroute, surrounded by potatoes, lard fumé, sausages and boiled meats, enough for a small army!

Thank goodness for Alsatian wines. They complement the heavy food so beautifully! Full and fruity, yet dry and highly acid, they're just the right thing to accompany a hearty choucroute. The fruitiness is assertive enough that it doesn't get lost next to the food. The acidity is high enough to clean the mouth and refresh the palate. It's as if the winemakers and the cooks got together one day and planned it all out! Yet, of course, they didn't. It just happened, through centuries of evolution, through living together side by side.

But wine is not the only partner for choucroute. Alsatian beer is worth considering. Usually light and pale, it is probably the more traditional way to wash down a plate of choucroute. Alsatians enjoy their beer, and depending on circumstances, will drink beer instead of wine. This is but another example of the region's German heritage.

Escargots à l'Alsacienne are well known throughout Alsace, and Alsatians are proud of them, but not because of their origins, nor the manner of raising them. The *raison d'être* for escargots, they admit, is their method of preparation! In other words, the important part of Escargots à l'Alsacienne is the *à l'Alsacienne*. This preparation involves taking the animal from its shell and cooking it in wine. The animal is then returned to its shell, ready to receive the important part: first, a concentrated essence of court bouillon made from cooking the escargots in wine, and second, a generous dose of fine herbs butter. Served piping hot, most will agree that the butter sauce is, indeed, the best part! And although locals often suggest drinking a Riesling with this dish, I'm not sure that I wouldn't prefer to postpone the wine to a course that would do it more justice, perhaps a dish of locally grown asparagus.

Asparagus is grown in the Lower Rhine area. It was first planted in 1873 in Hoerdt by a man named Heyler. Heyler had just come to Alsace from Algeria, where he had grown asparagus successfully for many years. He recognized that the conditions in Hoerdt were similar in enough ways to support the growth of the vegetable. So he planted it, and it grew. Since then, it has flourished, and has remained on much the same level as foie gras; namely a gourmet food.

In its preparation, Alsatians show their French heritage. They recommend cooking it a short time in water, draining it, then adding a sauce like hollandaise or mayonnaise. It is often served as a first course, by itself, so that its delicate flavour can be truly appreciated. Alsatians often drink a Sylvaner wine with asparagus. This is a good choice, I think. The earthiness so often apparent in this wine, balances well with the vegetal taste of the asparagus.

Frog legs are quite popular in Alsace, and in fact, date back to the thirteenth century. Apparently Strasbourg used to have a frog market next to its fish market! In the preparation of these delicacies, we see many French influenced recipes. A Mousseline de Grenouilles is served in some restaurants, such as the Auberge de l'Ill. But this is not the only way. Sautéed with garlic and parsley, the frog legs take on a Provençale tone. My favourite is Grenouilles au Riesling. As the name implies, the frog legs are simmered in Riesling until they become moist and tender. The wine is then reduced, concentrating its flavour, then made smooth and rich by the addition of cream. Fresh chives add zest and sparkle. An incredible dish!

As far as main courses are concerned, the pig reigns supreme in Alsace. In fact, its popularity probably dates back centuries, to the days of the Benedictine monks. It was, and still is, inexpensive to keep and it yields an incredible number and variety of products. There are roasted loins, chops or legs; or an infinite variety of sausages. Walking past a charcuterie in Alsace is an experience to remember: terrines and sausages display themselves proudly in row upon row of assorted colours, sizes and shapes.

Because of the abundance of pigs, game and fish, local cheeses are few and far between. There is only one well known cheese produced in Alsace: Muenster. But what a cheese! The Muenster of Alsace is gorgeous: it is soft in consistency, with a typically strong aroma. And how flavourful it is! Although some authorities suggest a Gewürztraminer with Muenster, I prefer a Muscat d'Alsace. With its clean, grapy flavour its a wonderful end to any meal!

But just in case you want more, Alsatians bake delicious desserts, most of which make wonderful use of local produce. A favourite example is any one of the fruit tarts seen in bakeries and shops. They are usually shallow pastry shells, filled with whatever fruit is available – apples, plums, berries or the like. All delicious. As it is said in Alsace, "the only thing better than a queutch tart...is two queutch tarts!"

And so ends our "typical" Alsatian fare. If there is such a thing. For it should be apparent that what belongs to Alsace is something like that bridal ritual – something old, something new, something borrowed...something that together spells out the essence of Alsace itself.

THE FOOD AND WINE OF BRITTANY AND ANJOU

Brittany is surrounded on three sides by water. As a result, a large part of its cuisine centers around fish and seafood.

For instance, there are oysters, Belon and Cancale and a multitude of different fish and crustaceans. Many go into a *Cotriade,* Brittany's answer to Bouillabaisse. This Breton fish stew is made from a large assortment of fish and shellfish. It may contain mullet, dory, angler fish, eel, whiting, mussels, and shrimp depending on what was caught that day. Onions, garlic and vegetables are first cooked gently in butter, for butter is the fat of Brittany. The fish is then added along with potatoes, which results in a typical Breton heartiness. These ingredients are simmered in a fish stock laced with Muscadet and/or Calvados, two beverages borrowed from surrounding areas but used often in Breton cooking. Perhaps it is the Muscadet which adds that special flavour to the *Cotriade* or perhaps the incomparably fresh fish, or maybe both. Interesting speculation, but once it is in your bowl, it hardly seems to matter!

Cotriade is only a beginning. Several well known and prestigious seafood dishes come from Brittany.

One is *Coquille St. Jacques.* Although this dish can be varied in as many ways as there are cooks, it usually consists of scallops served in a creamy sauce with the likely addition of a dry white wine.

Breton lobsters are famous, so it is not surprising that another seafood dish commonly attributed to Brittany is *Homard à l'Amoricaine,* the ancient name for Brittany being Amoricaine. The dish however, was actually created in Paris, and named *Homard à l'AmEricaine,* in honour of American tourists. Over time, however, both the name and the origin became twisted.

Not all the food in Brittany is fish. *Poitrine de Porc Frais* (Breast of Fresh Pork) is popular, as is *Lapin au Muscadet* (Rabbit cooked in Muscadet wine). The latter dish is almost predictable for the area, for small game like rabbit is readily available and so is Muscadet, a product of the Nantes area just south of Brittany.

According to Hubrecht Duijker in *The Great Wines of Burgundy,* the grape used in Muscadet originated in Burgundy, where it was known as Melon de Bourgogne. Experts found that its tendency to ripen early made it particularly well suited to the Nantes area which often experienced early autumn frosts.

The Muscadet area is a large one, covering the valley of the Sèvre and Maine rivers. As would be expected, the wine shows considerable variation in response to local microclimates. It is generally agreed that the best Muscadets come from Vallet and Saint Fiacre. Vallet, with its clay soil, produces robust wines. Saint Fiacre is hillier and sandier, producing a slightly softer wine.

The word Muscadet is derived from the French "musque," meaning musky. Although it is said that some Muscadets have a musky aroma, I personally find that their most outstanding feature is their clean acidity. They are light and dry, often with a hint of pétillance. A perfect summer wine and an excellent accompaniment to the seafoods that so dominate the local cuisine.

Brittany's geography does not lend itself to raising livestock. It is not surprising, then, that the area does not boast many local cheeses. The only one is Port Salut, a creamy whole milk cheese made in the Trappist monastery in Port du Salut.

One dessert in Brittany deserves special mention: *galettes* (griddle cakes) and *crêpes* (pancakes). These are made with either buckwheat or regular flour and may be filled with any number of sweet (or savoury) fillings. Sounds simple, perhaps, but anyone who has indulged in these Breton treats will tell you that this is the very soul of Breton food; simplicity and heartiness and an incredibly delicious blend of fresh, local ingredients.

As in Brittany, simplicity is also the most notable feature of Anjou cooking. That does not mean it lacks either flavour or ingenuity, it is merely not elaborate.

Perhaps the most outstanding gift that Anjou has made to French cuisine is *Beurre Blanc*. This is a rich, yet delicate tasting sauce whose main ingredient (as expected) is butter. Shallots, wine vinegar and a liberal dose of technique transform the butter into an incredible sauce. It is a classic accompaniment to non-oily, firm-fleshed fish.

On that most people agree. However, depending on what books you read or to whom you talk, you are liable to find different stories about the origin of *Beurre Blanc*. Some claim it originated in Anjou, others argue that it came from Brittany; after all, butter is plentiful there. Who knows? The sauce exists, and that's what matters. And how well its rich mellowness harmonizes with the light crisp white wines of the region.

But Anjou cooking is not just sauce. Like so many other areas of the country, Anjou has its fair share of fine charcuterie. The *rillauds* consist of large pieces of diced pork, macerated with coarse salt, then cooked in lard. Relatively heavy, they go well with the region's light crisp wines in that the wines cleanse the palate and refresh the mouth so that the next morsel of food can be better appreciated.

Other typical dishes include *Anguilles aux Pruneaux* (eels cooked with prunes), which is the local variation of the classic *Eels in Red Wine* seen in Bordeaux. *Pike with Beurre Blanc* uses the famous sauce of the region. Chicken is often served as a fricassée, stewed with mushrooms and onions in a local wine and finished with cream.

It should be apparent by now that there exists an intimately close relationship between the region's foods and wines. A closer look at the wines is thus in order.

Traditionally, the wines of Anjou were white, with most of them being sweet or semi-sweet. Only in the last ten to twenty years has a shift toward dry whites been noticeable.

The grape responsible for Anjou whites is the Chenin Blanc, which must make up at least 80 per cent. The other 20 per cent may be Sauvignon or Chardonnay, or a combination of both. These additions are helpful in creating a balanced and interesting wine, for Chenin Blanc alone can be quite acidic. Is this why traditional vinification in Anjou resulted in sweetish wines? Were vintners trying to balance the acidity? It is hard to say. In any case, white Anjou wines must be selected with care, for they show tremendous range of styles and tastes. Some are sweet, some are dry, others are in between. Some are meant to age, while others are to be drunk young.

There are red Anjou wines though they are relatively new to the wine scene. Most common is the Gamay Noir, an uncomplicated fruity wine best drunk young. The Cabernet Franc and/or Cabernet Sauvignon produce wines with a good fruity nose. These are normally lacking in tannin and therefore best consumed young, but are occasionally very tannic, needing ageing to mellow the tannins and bring out the fruit. Although pleasant, neither the Cabernet nor the Gamay Noir is what Anjou is famous for.

Rosé d'Anjou has that distinction. It is usually semi-sweet, and either pink or salmon-pink in colour. Most of the mass-produced rosé comes from the Groslot grape, with the addition of small amounts of many others. The result is good quality, fruity wine, pleasant but perhaps unremarkable.

The division of Anjou wines into such broad categories as white, red and rosé is incomplete to say the least. The Anjou area actually has more than twenty different appellations. Two areas deserve special mention: Coteaux du Layon and Saumur.

Coteaux du Layon, in the valley of the Layon river, for the most part produces sweet wines made exclusively from the Chenin Blanc grape. Hubrecht Duijker claims that this tendency toward sweet wines comes from the area's Dutch heritage. The Dutch, he explains, had a predilection for sweets and were interested in developing sweet wines, to which the long growing season and the abundance of sunshine lent itself.

Vintners today, as much as possible, encourage the growth of "pourriture noble" on their grapes. This has two effects: firstly, it dries out the grapes, concentrating their sugar and secondly, it brings about subtle changes in flavour. To allow for these developments, grapes are picked as late as possible, a practice that often means gambling with the weatherman.

A mature Coteaux du Layon is described beautifully by Duijker, as "...green gold in colour...teases the nose with a diversity of impressions (sweet fruit, nuts and spices like nutmeg) and delights the tongue with a fresh, almost austere sweetness..."

The wines of Coteaux du Layon go well with all kinds of fish, especially heavier ones. It also blends with poultry and feathered game. Oddly enough, I have even enjoyed Chinese dishes, such as Imperial Shrimp, with these wines!

The two most important and outstanding Coteaux du Layon wines have their own appellations: Quarts de Chaumes and Bonnezeaux.

Quarts de Chaumes is a small area south of the town of Chaumes, well protected from the northerly and westerly winds. Thus it has a slightly higher average temperature than its neighbours, resulting in well-ripened grapes. Most vineyards are harvested several times, only the ripest grapes being gathered each time round. If possible, grapes are allowed to "rot."

A good Quarts de Chaumes reaches its peak at ten to fifteen years of age. It enhances foods like chicken with cream sauces and can stand up well to blue cheese and foie gras.

Bonnezeaux is a district much the same size as Quarts de Chaumes, and similarly its grapes are picked when as ripe as possible and preferably affected by "pourriture noble." Winemaking techniques range from traditional fermentation in wood, to quicker fermentation in concrete. After five to ten years of ageing, a good Bonnezeaux is a truly delightful balance of elegance and fatness, with its fruit exploding in the mouth and lingering on and on.

Saumur is completely different from Coteaux du Layon. Its soil is calcareous, like that of Champagne. Furthermore, the area boasts miles and miles of underground chambers perfect for the maturing wine. Perhaps it makes sense, then, that many of the Saumur wines are sparkling. Saumur Mousseux and Crémant de Loire each have their own rules and regulations with regards to yield and production. The end products, although not like what you find in Champagne (for one thing, the grapes are different), are nevertheless delightful in their own right. A Crémant de Loire from Gratien and Meyer tasted recently showed good rich mousse, with pleasant balance between acid and fruit and an interesting hint of earthiness. Perfect with hors d'oeuvres before dinner.

It should be fairly obvious by now that I am biased toward the sweeter wines of the Anjou region. That does not mean that none of the area's newer style, drier wines are good; as the saying goes, ''to everything there is a season.'' Personally, though, I think that Chenin Blanc does benefit from some residual sugar. It seems to open up and blossom, developing a character and personality all its own.

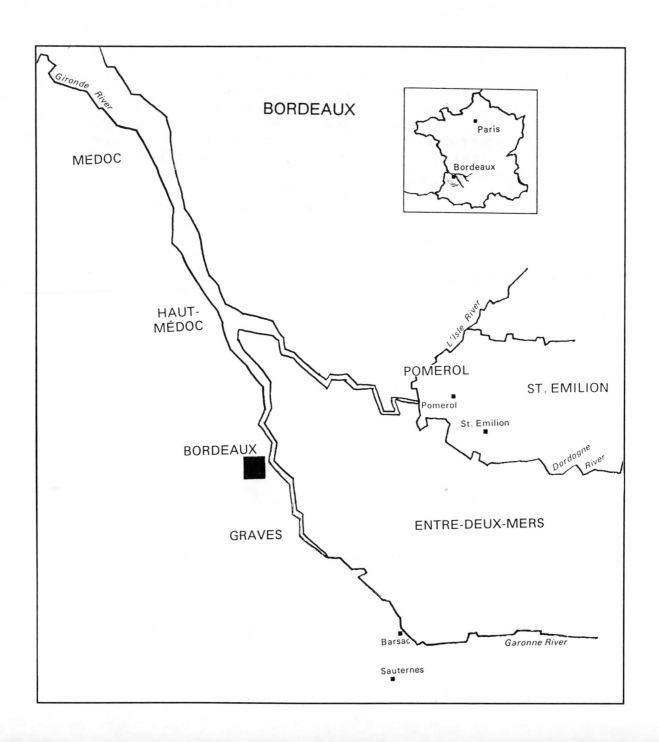

BORDEAUX

MEDOC

HAUT-
MÉDOC

POMEROL

ST. EMILION

Pomerol

St. Emilion

BORDEAUX

GRAVES

ENTRE-DEUX-MERS

Barsac

Sauternes

Gironde River

L'Isle River

Dordogne River

Garonne River

Paris

Bordeaux

THE FOOD AND WINE
OF BORDEAUX

Describing the wines of Bordeaux is no easy task. Volumes and volumes of material, written by Masters of Wine and world renowned experts, fill library shelves.

I would like to approach the wines of Bordeaux from a sensory point of view, to discuss how they smell, taste and feel in the mouth to enable you to make better purchasing decisions, plan better dinners, and generally increase your enjoyment. To cover this subject thoroughly would probably require another whole book. This next section is only intended to give you something to start with. In the end, your own taste experience is the best, and your own impressions the most valid.

With that in mind, it would be a good time to glance at the map on the opposite page. You will notice that the Bordeaux area is located in the southwest of France, with the Gironde, the Garonne, and the Dordogne rivers flowing through it. The four most important wine regions all lie remarkably close to the river beds. The Haut Médoc and Graves regions are located on the west bank of the Gironde; St. Emilion and Pomerol are located east of the river.

Wines from the haut Médoc and Graves are noticeably different from those of St. Emilion and Pomerol. This is partly due to differences in weather and soil, but even more, to the predominance of different grapes. Médoc and Graves contain a high proportion of Cabernet Sauvignon, while St. Emilion and Pomerol rely more heavily on Merlot. Understanding this, we can immediately predict that wines from the left bank will be somewhat harsh and tannic when young, and need long bottle ageing to soften and develop them. Those from the right bank, on the other hand, will be more supple wines, ready for drinking at an earlier age. To be more precise than this on a regional level is tricky, leaving one open to error, because there are great differences within as well as between regions. Nevertheless, some general tendencies can be delineated.

HAUT MÉDOC wines will be medium deep in colour. The nose and the flavour reflect the characteristics of the Cabernet Sauvignon grape which dominates its makeup. Depending on the particular wine and its age, you might notice things like red currants or blackcurrants on the nose (if you have ever smelled currants before!) or at least some kind of red or black berry-type of fruit. It will probably be mingled with a leathery or stalky odour if the wine is young and still tannic or perhaps a cedar or cigar box aroma if the wine is older. In the mouth, a well made Haut Médoc will give you a certain amount of astringency, good body, with a balance of fruit and oak. Good wines have many layers of taste and tend to linger in the mouth for a long time.

GRAVES wines tend to be more austere than the Haut Médocs. The soil of Graves contains a high proportion of sand and gravel, with some areas having a high iron content. This gives the wines a characteristic metallic aspect. The soil is also responsible for the kind of earthy or spicy/grassy character you sometimes taste in the Sauvignon Blancs, for which the region is well noted. The region's most famous red is Mission Haut Brion, a big, chewy, masculine wine that a colleague of mine often describes as "thick blood."

ST. EMILION wines are completely different. With the Merlot grape being so important in their makeup, St. Emilions are soft, round and generally more supple than Graves or Haut Médoc wines. The aroma is often very subtle, with a certain vegetal or barnyardy nose mingled with ripe, plummy fruit. In the mouth, they usually carry out the promise of the nose.

POMEROLS tend to have the same body as St. Emilions, but are often more aromatic. In the mouth, a mature Pomérol is rich and mouthfilling, with a silky texture, full of ripe plummy fruit from the Merlot grape. An instantly appealing wine, it tends to have good body, without too much tannin and acid.

Now that you are beginning to think that everything is quite simple, let me point out once again that these descriptions are meant mostly as generalizations, a starting point from which to orient your own experiences. You will find large variations in the wines within any of these regions, depending on the age, the individual style, and the vintage you are drinking.

You will notice this particularly in the Haut Médoc wines. As you move northward, the wines become deeper in colour, more tannic, less aromatic and less elegant. Similarly, the wines coming from vineyards closest to the river tend to show the greatest finesse, while those from vineyards further west are stronger and bigger.

The four best known sub-regions of the Haut Médoc, are St. Estèphe, Pauillac, St. Julien and Margaux.

St. Estèphe is the most northerly of the four. It is hotter than communes farther south and as a result, the grapes tend to build up a higher sugar concentration, yielding wines with higher alcohol content. The wines are heavy and dense, big and full-bodied, with a high tannin content and an earthy bouquet. As would be expected from these characteristics, they are slow to mature and are therefore very long lived.

This description is especially true of St. Estèphe's older style wines. They are heavy and astringent when young, and fairly difficult to drink. Only after considerable ageing do they mellow and allow their fruit to blossom amidst a background of tannin.

However recent years have seen changing trends, perhaps in response to cashflow or perhaps in reaction to the public's demand for ready to drink wines. A few vintners are now producing smooth wines lower in tannin than is traditional for the area. The majority of St. Estèphe wines are somewhere in between the traditional and light. Typical St. Estèphes, such as those from Calon-Ségur and Cos d'Estournel, show deep colour, some astringency, with a rich and assertive taste and a long, firm finish.

Pauillac lies just to the south of St. Estèphe. According to our generalization about north-south characteristics, we would expect Pauillac wines to also be big and powerful, but perhaps with just a bit more breed and bouquet. Such is the case. Pauillac wines tend to be rich and regal. When mature, they exhibit an intense Cabernet Sauvignon nose, of the cedar/cigar box variety. In the mouth, they make their presence felt in no uncertain terms, with good body and firm structure. Although they are full of fruit, the overall impression is somewhat harder and more assertive than, let's say, a St. Julien or a Margaux. But Pauillacs age superbly, and show great depth of flavour.

The real claim to fame of Pauillac is its three first growths – Mouton, Latour and Lafite. All fall within its bounds, each being typically Pauillac, yet at the same time, completely individual. Mouton is usually a big, heavyweight wine that Michael Broadbent describes as "the Tchaikovsky of Médoc." Lafite, on the other hand is described by experts as being more understated, more gentlemanly. Latour is known for its strength and depth of flavour. What an incredible trio for Pauillac to claim.

South of Pauillac is *St. Julien*. Its soil is gravelly, like that of Margaux, but with more clay. Perhaps that is why it is said that St. Julien combines the firmness of Pauillac with the soft elegance of Margaux, uniting the best features found separately in the other communes. This is meant as a compliment. Personally, I am very much of an individualist, and I think that this reference to St. Julien is somewhat unfair. For St. Julien is not a melting pot; it is itself – charming, personable, intensely likeable.

Typically, a St. Julien wine has a perfumed nose, reminiscent of berries. In the mouth, it tastes above all of fruit, lots and lots of it. For people who enjoy a fruity wine, St. Julien is the route to heaven. But St. Julien is much more than simple fruit; if well made, it will be round and plush, yet have enough tannin and acidity to enhance the fruitiness and make it more interesting and complex. When mature the flavour of currants and berries will mingle intimately with shades of cedar and cigar box, giving layer upon layer of nuances for which to return time and time again.

As in other communes, there are differences in style evident between different châteaux. For instance, Beychevelle and Léoville-LasCases are elegant and highly perfumed, while Lagrange and Léoville-Barton are more full-bodied but somewhat less refined. Many experts suggest that the terrain has a lot to do with producing these variations, pointing out that finesse and bouquet decrease as vineyards get farther away from the river and closer to the plateau of St. Laurent on the west. How noticeable these differences are depends on how much you have tasted and, to a certain extent, what particular vintage you are tasting. Even your mood and the food you are eating (if any) will play a role. But none can be defined as good or bad; it is more a case of what you yourself prefer. I tend to like most of the St. Juliens, but that should be quite apparent by now!

Not that *Margaux* isn't fantastic, mind you. In fact, Margaux wines more than any other seems to leave writers speechless. When words do come, they are usually superlatives. Hugh Johnson describes Margaux wines as "having a sweet, haunting perfume," and being "soft, supple and very elegant in the mouth." David Peppercorn in *Bordeaux* writes: "its wines are delicately perfumed in youth and this perfume fills out and deepens in the years of maturity. On the palate, although lacking somewhat in body, they fill the mouth with flavour at once delicate, refined and subtle, full of nuances and finesse."

Finesse and bouquet, soft flavour, classic elegance – that's Margaux.

* * * *

With such an array of fine wines to choose from, how in the world do you choose intelligently.

The best place to start is probably to try representative selections. Organize a tasting that gives you the opportunity to taste one wine from each of the four major sub-regions (Haut Médoc, Graves, Pomerol and St. Emilion) and, if possible, at another time, wines representing the different communes of Haut Médoc (St. Estèphe, Pauillac, St. Julien and Margaux). For it is only by tasting and discussing that you begin to form preferences and impressions of what the different wines are like to you.

Aside from preference (and availability!) there is the matter of whether you are planning to drink the wine alone or with food. Personally, I find many Bordeaux wines – even the St. Juliens that I so enjoy – difficult and/or tiring to drink alone. Food seems to enhance them tremendously and in turn, they seem to enhance the food.

The same rules as always apply. The most essential, of course, is to avoid overpowering. That means don't match a St. Estèphe to a light, delicate veal dish. Steak au Poivre is probably a better bet. And if Steak au Poivre is your dinner, watch the pepper. Too much can overpower even the most powerful Bordeaux. The older the Bordeaux and the more full of subtleties it is, the more you have to watch what you pair it with.

There are some classic combinations; lamb with Pauillac, for instance, and most Médocs with game. Then, of course there is beef. In North America, we tend to think of Bordeaux primarily in terms of its great wines. We don't often ponder over its food. Before going any further we might consider what foods are found in the Bordeaux region itself, and who would know better about what to eat with those wines than the people of Bordeaux.

If asked about Bordeaux food, many of us would think first of Sauce Bordelaise. We may be tempted to think of Bordeaux cuisine as a succession of wine sauces or at least, very haute cuisine – very buttery, rich and very "French."

In fact, that's not true. Not everything has a sauce, and not everything uses butter. There are as many dishes that represent *cuisine paysanne* as *haut cuisine*. Food in Bordeaux is meant to enhance the subtleties of its wines, not compete.

What then, is the Bordelais style? What can you expect from a food prepared "à la Bordelaise?"

There seem to be several interpretations of this term. To many Bordelais residents, "à la Bordelaise" refers to the presence of parsley, accompanied by either shallots or garlic – those further north using shallots and those further south using garlic. To others "à la Bordelaise" means the use of *cèpes*; those large, fleshy mushrooms native to the area. Another interpretation is seen in classic French cooking. Here, "à la Bordelaise" refers to a garnish of artichokes and potatoes. Although artichokes are certainly native to the Bordelais region, this garnishing is not one of the local traditions.

Then there is *Entrecôte Bordelaise* – a story in itself. In North America an order of *Entrecôte Bordelaise* will get you a piece of beef bathed in a Sauce Bordelaise. The latter is prepared by reducing a red wine, always Bordeaux, with shallots, then adding this reduction to a basic brown sauce. The result is mouthwatering – a beautiful harmony between wine and food.

Although it is conceivable that a Bordeaux restaurant will give you the same thing, purists will argue with this interpretation and tell you that true *Entrecôte Bordelaise* can only be experienced close to a vineyard. Food writer Adrian Bailey, in *The Taste of France,* explains that an *Entrecôte Bordelaise* is prepared by grilling a thick steak (traditionally not beef, but vineyard rodents!) over prunings from the Cabernet Sauvignon vines, with a few Merlot twigs thrown in at the last moment to give smoke, and enhance flavour. Chopped shallots garnish the finished steak.

Personally, I wouldn't argue over interpretations. I would rather try them both although, I must confess, a preference for beef over vineyard rodents! Whichever the source of protein, though, Entrecôte Bordelaise is one good example of how the cuisine of Bordeaux relies on local resources, namely, its vines.

Other supplies are furnished by the woods around the Gironde and the forests of the Landes. In the fall, these areas are the source of *cèpes* those fat, fleshy mushrooms mentioned earlier. They are found wild near oaks and pines, and are undoubtedly the cause of much "sickness" as the pressure to spend an afternoon picking mushrooms surpasses the desire to work. There seems to exist a wealth of folklore about both picking procedures and cooking methods. Generally, *cèpes* are cooked in a casserole with oil, then drained and refried in fresh oil with parsley and garlic. Apparently, the first cooking serves to remove those compounds in the *cèpes* which could cause bitterness and the second frying adds the complementary flavour of parsley and garlic. Yes, the people of the Landes region actually use garlic, not shallots, and oil, not butter. Here we see the influence of the south and in fact, a look at a map will remind you that the Bordelais is farther south than you might think.

The forests furnish more than mushrooms. Game is also hunted; partridge, quail, pheasant, deer, hare and many more. *Civest* of stewed venison are popular, as are *salmis* of game. The latter refers to poultry cooked in the kitchen, then finished in a showy style at the table. Other game is roasted over an open fire.

Lamb is raised in the Landes region, as well as in Pauillac. It is often milk fed and killed young in order to create exceptionally tender and tasty meat. Roasted, then garnished with the delicate flavour of parsley and shallots, a rack of lamb makes the perfect accompaniment to the wines of Pauillac.

Looking at this abundance of local game and also lamb, one can see why those classic combinations of lamb and Pauillac, game and Médoc came to be. Surely, they do go well together. The strong taste of these meats are complemented by the assertive fruit of the wines. But more than this, they simply are found close enough to each other that local residents tend to use them together, which ultimately accounted for the development of local cuisine before the days of jumbo jets and the food importing business. So if the Bordelais was not cow country (and it's not), then no matter how well beef and Médoc might go together, you will never see it on lists of local food-wine matchups. At least, not the traditional ones. This, of course, doesn't prevent you from making your own matches – you might as well take advantage of what you have at your disposal. The point here is simply that many classic combinations do make sense and can be explained by the geography, the agriculture and the resources of a region.

You might be thinking by now that Bordelais food is only meat. A somewhat strange, but definitely local, specialty involves lamprey found in the area's rivers. They are cooked in one of the region's red wines, similar to what is done in the Lyon area of Burgudy. If just the idea of lampreys in red wine turns off your appetite (or even if it doesn't), you might be interested to know that for Henry I, they were a favourite. In fact, legend has it that he died from overeating them!

If you prefer fish other than lamprey, go to the south of the Bordelais, to the Arachon basin. There you will find a delectable assortment of oysters and crustaceans, a nice accompaniment to the Sauvignon Blancs that Bordeaux has to offer.

But Sauvignon Blanc, although very nice is not that for which Bordeaux is famous. Bordeaux's red wines are its claim to fame, representing luxury and opulence; for many, the quintessence of what wine is all about. To go with this, one needs not only the simplicity and the subtleness, as we have seen so far, but also a matching luxury. And luxury we see! For the Bordelais, along with its neighbouring region of Perigord, is the home of both foie gras and truffles. Foods that even to locals are as important as the region's best wines. And how well the rich fatness of the foie gras is complemented by the assertive and tannic fruit of the Cabernet Sauvignon. Each is strong and lush, yet completely different in its mouthfeel. Each gives the mouth something the other does not have; the wine a firmness, the foie gras, a fatness. Each alone is tiring, yet together the two can go on and on forever.

Yes, that is the kind of harmony that is the essence of Bordeaux, lush, yet well structured, simple, yet full of nuances; individual, yet classic.

THE FOOD AND WINE OF GERMANY

"Most of us think of German food as an endless succession of sausages and sauerkraut, working up to a grand climax of sauerbraten and dumplings, with every dish washed down by great steins of beer hoisted by hefty maidens while the band plays oom-pa-pa."

Nika Hazelton,
The Cooking of Germany

To a certain extent, this is true. Sausages and sauerkraut come in endless varieties and together occupy a cornerstone in German cuisine. As for meat and potatoes (or dumplings), they're everywhere: you can have meat and potatoes three times a day without even trying! Not exactly the lightest cuisine in the world. But not boring: the Germans have created an amazingly diverse cuisine from a very few basic ingredients.

The potato is one such ingredient. However, the Germans were not always potato lovers. During the time of Frederick the Great, many European nations were cultivating and enjoying the potato – but not Germany. Frederick, who must have been a potato lover himself, realized this and arranged a kind of "shot-gun wedding" between the potato and the German farmers. In typical Frederick the Great style, he issued a formal decree for everyone to plant potatoes – which he supplied –and even went so far as to station soldiers in peasants' fields to ensure that people followed orders.

Today, there are a multitude of different kinds of potatoes grown in the country, especially in lower Saxony and the Palatinate. The ingenuity that Germans apply to the potato is truly remarkable. As a simple side dish, it can be boiled, baked, steamed or mashed. Fried potatoes are also popular and can be garnished with bacon, ham, onions or cheese. A favourite Rhineland recipe cooks potatoes with apples in a dish called "Heaven and Earth", the potatoes represent earth and the apples, heaven. Potatoes may also be served as a soufflé, as potato pancakes, as a multitude of salads, as a creamy potato soup – or even combined with flour to make potato noodles or potato dumplings.

Dumplings brings up another important category of recipes, for dumplings "are to German cuisine what pasta is to the Italian" (Mimi Sheraton, *The German Cookbook*) –especially in the south. And just as Italian pasta can vary tremendously, so do dumplings vary in size, shape and texture, depending on the food and/or liquid they are meant to accompany. Some are served in clear broth, while others accompany the main course. Some contain meat and *are* the main course. Others are served with fruit sauces as dessert. Whatever their place in the menu, dumplings are usually cooked in liquid and tend to expand greatly during the cooking process. A relative of mine – who shall remain nameless – once served a dumpling the size of a soccer ball. Apparently she had taken all the raw mixture and formed it into one ball (which looked small enough at the time), then put it into a pot of soup to cook. Soon the cover of the pot started rising...and what was probably the world's most enormous dumpling was carved at the table. Seriously, though, dumplings represent a delicious use of simple and economic ingredients. The liver dumplings so popular in the south of Germany are a particularly savoury example, often served in clear broth.

Soup is one of the nicest parts of German cookery, especially if you're a soup lover. It is seen in many forms, and can be made from literally anything available. Although clear broths are common, many soups are thick, stick to the ribs type: goulash soup is a meal in itself, often seen in Bavaria. Lentil soup, which may be served with sliced sausage in it, is also filling enough to be a main course.

Most soups make use of local food resources. Hunter's soup features the many local mushrooms found in wooded areas. Asparagus soup is offered in the spring in the Rhine valley just south of Mainz, when local asparagus is in season. Potato soup is seen in many parts of the country, as is onion soup. And so on goes the list . . . German resourcefulness will make creative use of whatever is available.

The same holds true in preparing meat. And let me tell you, not even Americans eat meat as often as the Germans – or in such enormous quantities. Only in Germany does a restaurant serve you seconds all for the same price!

Although the pig is the most important source of meat in Germany, good use is made of veal and beef. Variety meats are well used and are often considered as delicacies.

Whether the meat is pork or beef, its most common preparation is as the *braten,* or roast. Depending on the particular cut, it might be cooked open in the oven or, more probably, browned then cooked covered with a small amount of liquid. The latter is favoured for two reasons: first, it allows for the use of less tender, less expensive cuts of meat, and secondly, it produces delicious juices that go well with the potatoes or dumplings that will probably be served with it. Because of the type of meat and its method of cooking, it will never be rare, but you can be sure it will be tender and juicy. The gravy will often be served as is, or possibly enriched with wine, cream or spices.

Pork is served in a variety of different ways. Chops, croquettes and stews can each have a number of different garnishes, either savoury or sweet. In Westphalia, some pigs are fed on the acorns of the region's large oak trees, then slaughtered and the meat lightly smoked to produce a ham not too different from Italy's prosciutto or Spain's serrano ham.

When it comes to sausages, the Germans again demonstrate diversity. Most sausages can be eaten either hot or cold, but some are always eaten hot and others are always eaten cold. Some are spicy, some are delicate, some raw, some cured, and the names all have many syllables, so really, you have to live with them (stomach, watch out!) to begin to understand them.

Schnitzels – thin filets of veal – are easier to understand (and digest!). They are usually pounded thin, often breaded, then fried. They may be stuffed with cheese and/or ham, or given a sauce such as mushrooms and sour cream (just when you thought you were going to eat something light!).

Poultry comes into its own in Germany with duck and goose. These are both easy and inexpensive to raise and tend to be surprisingly meaty. They are usually braised rather than roasted in order to produce more flavourful, more tender meat. Stuffings are varied, but often include fruits which are an attractive complement to the gamey flavour of the meat. In fact, the venison and other game meats so common in the Black Forest region are often prepared in a similar manner: braised, with fruits such as red currants added to the gravy. A nice marriage of opposing flavours, perhaps stemming from the availability of fruits and berries, coupled with the Germans' love of sweets.

And sweets they get! No matter where you go in the country, there's always a bakery with not only breads of all kinds, but cookies, cakes, and pastries that boggle the mind! Apples, berries, cherries and chocolate all find their way into dazzling delights. Whether in the form of cookies, cakes or strudels, they are rich, sweet, and in a word, fantastic.

The German sweet tooth has found its way into winemaking as well, for many of the country's most prized wines contain a great amount of residual sugar. However, even the sweetest of them are not cloying or heavy. Because of their cold weather origin, they tend to have a high degree of acidity. This balance between sugar and acid gives the wines of Germany a refreshing, often elegant aspect.

It might seem strange that a country which produces such refreshing white wines should eat such a heavy meat and potatoes type of diet. The two don't seem to match.

Actually, they do! Good German wines, although white, have enough bouquet, enough intensity of fruit and enough acidity to stand up to any meat! The acidity is especially important here. It serves to cleanse the palate and refresh the mouth – cutting through the heaviness of the food, serving as a fresh, lively counterpoint. As long as the wine has these characteristics, it serves its function during mealtime with remarkable ease and grace. But it's certainly not the focal point of a meal. The serious drinking only begins *after* dinner. You might be offered a Spätlese and gradually work your way up into Auslese or Beerenauslese, which could take hours, or course. German restaurants never have two sittings – once a table is occupied, it's occupied for the evening. That's how the elite of German wines are best enjoyed: alone and unhurried, after dinner.

Let me point out, though, that not all white wines were created equal. In other words, not all German wine is Liebfraumilch. On the contrary, German wines exhibit a tremendous amount of variation, stemming from differences in grape variety, micro-climate, and residual sugar. A look at some of the country's wine-producing areas should explain this more fully.

The Mosel-Saar-Ruwer

Although the Mosel winegrowing area can be divided into five subregions, the Middle Mosel, the Saar and the Ruwer are the most noted.

The Mosel has some of the steepest hillsides in Germany. The most desired are those sheltered from the wind and facing south toward the sun. For the "grapevine," say the Germans, "is a child of the sun, it loves the hills and hates the wind." And especially here in the Mosel, one of the most northerly winegrowing districts in Europe, an area where the climate is far from ideal.

The slate soil is a tremendously important aspect of the area. It is all along the river banks and is chopped up and spread beneath the vines like a kind of topsoil. During the day it reflects the sun's rays upward on the vines, and at the same time stores some of the daytime heat. During the night it releases this heat and warms the air around the vines. The overall effect is to moderate the temperature around the vines. The reflection of sun off the river in the daytime adds to this effect.

Riesling occupies more than half of the vineyards in this area. The Müller-

Thurgau grape has been introduced onto some of the lower slopes, and now accounts for about 23 per cent of plantings.

The Riesling wines of the area are the most important and well known, though they vary from spot to spot within the region.

The Saar wines are starkly masculine, with the hard cold winters and flinty soil producing a steely wine. The Ruwer wines, on the other hand, are softer and friendlier, more feminine in nature, with a greater bouquet. The wines of the middle Mosel are generally described as delicate, flowery, fragrant, and elegant, possessing a lively and refreshing acidity.

One of the most famous places in the Middle Mosel is Piesport, a tiny town located at the base of a vast steep "bowl" of vineyards on the north bank of the Mosel. The most sought after vineyard is in the centre of the bowl, facing almost due south and catching the most sun reflections off the river. Its name is Goldtropfchen, meaning "little drops of gold." In a good year it can be the greatest of Mosel wines!

The Rheingau

Perhaps the most elite of German winegrowing regions, the Rheingau is situated at the base of the Taunus mountains between where the Rhine turns west at Mainz and where it turns north once again at Bingen.

The Taunus mountains act as a shelter, giving the region cold winters and warm summers. An average rainfall of 55 mm and more than average sunshine, part direct and part reflected off the Rhine, all contribute to making the Rheingau a great winegrowing region, where Riesling is truly king.

The soil contributes as well. Quartzite and slate in the higher sites produce a pithy, elegant wine. The loam and clay soil of the valley result in a more full, robust wine.

Compared to other German wine growing areas, the Rheingau is small, yet the number of taste nuances in the wines is astounding! Each little village and each vineyard has its own unique characteristics, which experts can often pinpoint quite exactly. For example, Hochheimers are full and fruity with a trace of earthiness; Rauenthalers are distinguished by their spicy fruitiness; Eltvillers are well balanced and pleasing; Hattenheimers are full of finesse and delicacy; Steinbergers are masculine and forthright; Johannisbergers possess elegance and distinction; and so on.

In fact, even within a single vineyard there can be vast differences! For in the Rheingau especially, and to a certain degree all over Germany, a single vineyard can be owned by many producers: much like Clos de Vougeot in Burgundy. So it is important, if not vital, to know the producer of a wine. Many German experts suggest, in fact, that your choice of a wine be governed first by the producer, and secondly by the vineyard. They claim that a good producer can make a good wine almost anywhere, but a bad producer can spoil wine from even the best vineyard. So get to know your producers!

The Rheinhessen

The Rheinhessen can be pictured as a somewhat rectangular area, bound on the east and north by the Rhine River, and on the west by the Nahe River. It is sheltered by the Hunsruck mountains to the west and the Taunus mountains to the north and east.

The mountains protect against the cold winds, helping to keep the average temperature at favourable levels. They also affect the precipitation pattern of the area. Although the total rainfall is low, its distribution is made to order, being heaviest early in the growing season, and lightest during September and October: perfect for producing intense, full-flavoured grapes.

The soil contributes, too. Although there is much diversity, a good portion of the Rheinhessen soil is red sandstone or slate – both important for their high mineral content and their ability to hold the warmth of the sun.

Traditionally, the Sylvaner grape dominated this area. Since the war, it has lost popularity, because, as one grower explains, "sweet Sylvaner is dull." Some growers have responded by replanting with Müller-Thurgau, while others have tried producing a dry Sylvaner, which they claim is more interesting and well suited to the region. I tasted a Sylvaner Spätlese trocken from 1979 and found it dry and elegant, full-bodied, having good balance and an interesting earthy aspect. Hardly dull! However, wines like this are not typical.

Riesling wines, flowery on the nose and fruity in the mouth, are more common. The most famous are those from the Nierstein, Bingen and Oppenheim areas; also from the area around "The Church of Our Lady" in Worms, which yield the world-famous "Liebfraumilch" wine. Each of these shares a common Riesling character, and each has its own nuances given by the soil and the condition in which it grows. Yet as a whole they are typically Rheinhessen, soft and full, easy to enjoy.

The Rheinpfalz

Lying along the foot of the Donersberg, Haardt and Wasgau hills is the belt of vineyards which form collectively the largest wine producing area of Germany. The vineyards are located along the lower slopes of the hills, facing east over a plain. No other German winegrowing area has as large and as uninterrupted a stretch of vineyards as does the Rheinpfalz.

The region is one of the most fertile and climatically favourable in the country, with more sunshine than any other area, accompanied by sufficient, but not too much, rainfall. The grapes thus attain a great degree of ripeness, and there is hardly a year where there are no late harvest wines.

The soils of the area display great variety, including loam sandstone, granite, slate and more. Each type has its own heat holding capacity, its own mineral composition, and its own fertility. Each type confers its own special character on the wine produced from its vines.

Müller-Thurgau takes up about 24 per cent of the Rheinpfalz vineyard area, yielding wines that are smooth and fruity, with a slight muscat-like bouquet. The Riesling, the Sylvaner, and the Kerner follow, each accounting for 10 to 13 per cent of the total vineyard area. A specialty of the area is Gewürztraminer, which, due to its poor yield accounts for only a small part of the harvest, but is sold by most quality conscious vintners.

The Nahe

The Nahe region begins along the banks of the Nahe River at the Bingen, where it joins the Rhine. It stretches through into the valleys and tributaries of the Nahe, the Guldenbach, the Grafenbach, the Glan and the Alsenz.

The climate in this area favours viticulture, with an annual temperature of ten degrees celsius, and over 1500 hours of sunshine. This compares well with other areas of the country.

About one third of the vineyards are covered with Müller-Thurgau, with Sylvaner coming next.

Writers often describe Nahe wines as having a combination of Mosel and Rheingau characteristics. One says "they draw their substance, body and fruitiness from the Rhine, their elegance and breeding from the Mosel." Hugh Johnson claims that the Nahe wines "seem to capture all the qualities one loves best in German wine. They are very clean and grapy, with all the intensity of the Riesling, like a good Mosel or Saar wine. At the same time they have some of the full flavour of the Rheingau."

Perhaps the only thing that may be said with any confidence is that there is a great variation in styles and tastes in Nahe wines, arising partly from grape type and partly from the different microclimates in the region. Rudolf Knoll's nickname "Tasting room of German Wine Lands" *German Wine Review* 1982 is truly appropriate!

* * * *

In conclusion, I can only stress again the word "diversity": for both the wine and the food of Germany are varied, reflecting local resources, local geography and local customs. But there is also a certain harmony and balance in German gastronomy. As a whole, the food is hearty and simple; the wines are fragrant and fruity, so refreshingly acidic. An unusual, but interesting balance.

THE FOOD AND WINE OF ITALY

Mention of Italian cooking usually conjures up visions of veal, sliced thinly, sautéed quickly in a skillet and served with a sauce made just as quickly in the same skillet, with the help of a local wine and perhaps fresh vegetables.

Research shows that this style of cooking is not haphazard. It was developed not so much by whim as by need. Historically, Italy has never enjoyed the luxury of an abundant fuel supply. She could not afford to develop recipes which needed a long, hot fire. Besides, the climate in most of the country is warm, so cooking quickly was probably welcomed.

The popularity of veal can be understood in terms of this scenario. Thinly sliced scallopini cook in minutes and blend well with almost any wine or vegetable garnish. As an added bonus the meat comes from a relatively small animal which could therefore be finished quickly enough to remain fresh even before the days of refrigeration. Freshness is, in fact, a key to Italian cooking.

This desirable characteristic is provided by nature. In Italy no point of land is more than 150 miles from the sea with the following consequences: (1) an endless variety and amount of fish and seafood and (2) an evenly warm climate. The latter helps to provide the country with a long enough growing season in every region to furnish a rich supply of lush fruits and vegetables. Fruits, of course, include grapes and there is hardly an area of the country without a local wine industry.

So two threads run through all of Italian cuisine: (1) a quick skillet-based style of cooking and (2) a lush supply of raw ingredients, especially fish and seafood, fruits and vegetables, and wine.

At the same time as this seeming unity however, there exists an endless diversity to Italian cuisine. Seldom can a person find one sure and certain method for preparing any recipe. Each village and often each household, has its own secret and seemingly authentic procedure. Take, for example, a dish like lasagna; ask for it in one hundred different places and you will get one hundred different versions. The same applies to fish stew, Bolognese sauce or anything else you try.

77

This is partly due to geography. Italy is mountainous. Mountains are effective barriers and tend to isolate villages and towns. As a result, customs and habits become ingrained. Local needs and resources provide the raw materials and local wisdom provides the methodology.

The personality and heritage of a local population is by inference important. In this respect, Italy is again fragmented. The north of Italy can trace its roots back to the Etruscans. The south, to the Greeks. Each of these groups had its own culture and personality and each its own favourite foods. For example, the Etruscans introduced *polenta,* (corn meal porridge) still common in northern Italy. The Greeks brought with them *fish soups and stews,* still seen in innumerable variations along the coast of southern Italy.

The north and south are different, not only from an historical and ethnic point of view, but also from a topographical, agricultural and economic perspective. The north has enough pasturage and wealth to raise dairy cattle, so female animals are kept for their milk, while males are slaughtered young for their meat (called *vitello*). The south is drier and poorer. It therefore raises only small amounts of cattle, relying more on fish (which is plentiful and cheap) as a source of protein.

It is not surprising, then, that the north and south use different forms of fat in their cooking. The north, with its relative abundance of dairy cattle, uses butter. The south uses olive oil, for olive trees grow easily even in dry soil.

Pasta is common to both regions but in different forms. In the north, it tends to be made with egg and is usually flat in shape. In the south, because of the relative poverty, pasta is made without egg. As a result, it is stiffer and drier, well suited to tubular shapes. The sauce put on the pasta, although highly variable, will be creamier in the north as in Alfredo or Cardinale or contain an abundance of meat, as in Bolognese. In the south it might be based on oil and contain an assortment of seafood.

We can see now that it is very difficult to delineate one style which is "Italian cooking." More appropriate would be visits to specific regions. Piedmont and Tuscany will be the two we concentrate on.

Piedmont

Gastronomically, Piedmont does not have one well defined cuisine. Its gastronomic borders do not match its political borders. In essence, Piedmont is two different cuisines: (1) the cuisine of the cities and the southern plain, and (2) the cuisine of the mountains (north of Turin).

In Turin, cooking is more an emulation of French cuisine than anything else.

Although delicious, it tends to show little "local" character. Mountain cuisine, on the other hand, makes use of local resources and individualism so characteristic of mountain people. Geography and climate have played a role too; cold mountain weather brings a desire for hearty food. Furthermore, without ovens (as many were for a long time), Piedmont cooking relied upon an open fire over which either a kettle or a frypan could be used, so dishes like soups and stews became common.

The most uniquely Piedmontese food is the *white truffle,* found in the region around Alba. These exotic fungi grow around the roots of oak trees, willows, poplars and other trees, and usually at an altitude of between thirteen hundred and two thousand feet. In France, the hog is the chief truffle hunter; in Piedmont it is the dog specially trained for the task. Hunting is usually done at night because then the odour of the truffles is stronger, even when they are a foot underground. Apparently, (I've never had the honour) white truffles have a stronger taste than black ones.

Truffles are a key ingredient in many local dishes. Perhaps the best known is *Fonduta.* This is exactly what it sounds like; an Italian version of cheese fondu, but with a difference. Fontina cheese, coming from the Valle d'Aosta, is blended not with wine as in the French and Swiss versions, but with a mixture of butter, milk and egg yolks. Finally, the Italian concoction is crowned with a layer of thinly sliced white truffles. Omitting this last touch apparently robs the dish of all its character. So if you can manage to find white truffles, by all means use them. Then serve the Fonduta like the Piedmontese do, either in small bowls, like soup, or poured over pieces of *polenta.*

Another uniquely Piedmont dish is *Bagna Cauda,* literally meaning "hot bath." It is made by heating together a mixture of butter and oil. Chopped garlic is added, along with finely chopped anchovies. If available, some white truffle is added as well. The mixture is served hot and used as a dip for vegetables.

Rice is popular in Piedmont as might be expected seeing that it grows so well in the Po Valley. Seldom eaten by itself, rice is enhanced with meat sauce and (yes) truffles or chick peas and tomato sauce. Sometimes it is boiled in milk, then served with grated cheese; all hearty, stick-to-the-ribs mountain fare.

But rice does not exclude the presence of pasta in Piedmont. Rings of egg pasta, called *agnolotti,* are found stuffed with mixtures of meat and spinach, seasoned with nutmeg. *Tagliatelle* is often served with a meat sauce containing white truffle (there we go again). Lasagna is served as well, with each cook in each town having his or her special variation.

Meat and poultry dishes reflect local resources in many ways. Heavy use of large kettles over open fires means that stews are popular. *Bolloto Misto* is a mixture of beef, chicken and other meats cooked together with onions, cabbage and potatoes. *Tripe Beef Braised in Barolo* is a natural in the area, marrying the flavours of food and wine in what you might describe as Italy's version of Boeuf Bourguignon. (Doesn't every country have one?)

That brings us (conveniently) to the subject of wines and Piedmont is a particularly good region to look at. It is often called the fine wine leader of Italy. It is a region of extremes; on one hand, you see the giants manufacturing vermouths and spumantes for mass markets all over the world and on the other hand, you see small family wineries producing small amounts of expensive wine aged for years before being sold, and then only locally.

As in any wine-producing region, the effect of geography and climate is important. In Piedmont the influence of the Alps is strong. They line the northern part of the region and give the area both a hot growing season and frequent autumn fog.

The grape which makes some of Piedmont's most famous wines is, in fact, a translation of the word "fog", namely Nebbiolo. From it come the Barolo and Barbaresco wines.

Barolo was one of the first of Italy's wines to be elevated to the distinctive DOCG (Denominazione di Origine Controllata e Garantita) status. For a wine to be called "Barolo," it must be made completely from Nebbiolo grapes grown in a small, specifically defined area south of the Tanaro River and must be aged a minimum of two years in wood before being bottled. A "riserva" is usually aged for four years. If the word "speciale" appears on the label, the wine has been aged in wood for more than five years. However, the influence of the wood is less than one might think because the barrels used to age Barolo are larger than the type used in Bordeaux.

Hugh Johnson compares Barolo to Châteauneuf-du-Pape. Indeed Piedmont lies on much the same latitude as the Côtes du Rhône. This is a good starting point as it gives a clue what kind of fullness and body to expect. But Barolo is Barolo, and cannot be justly compared to any French wine. As would be expected from the warm climate, Barolo is a fairly alcholic wine of usually twelve to fifteen per cent. Its nose is sometimes tarry, sometimes earthy, with a noticeable amount of cooked fruit. In the mouth it is big, powerful and full-bodied, with the components of the nose coming through to the palate and ending with a dry tannic finish.

Barbaresco is similar. It too comes from Nebbiolo grapes grown in a defined area south of the Tanaro River, in this case near the town of Barbaresco (hence its name). However, in this case the grapes grow lower down on the slopes than do those destined for Barolo and the fog affects the vines sooner, resulting in a drier, less fully ripened wine. The wine tends to be lower in alcohol than Barolo, less tannic, and earlier to mature. It is often quite dry and full-bodied, but somewhat less austere than Barolo. Like Barolo it goes well with red meat and game.

Wines not measuring up to the DOCG standards for Barolo or Barbaresco are usually put into a varietal wine, with the label simply saying Nebbiolo. In certain communes (e.g. Gattinara) the wine is given the commune name instead of the grape name. If the grapes all come from a specific area, for instance, Alba, then that name is attached to the varietal name, as in Nebbiolo d'Alba. As a matter of fact, the Nebbiolo from Alba is considered to be one of the best of the Nebbiolo varietals. The wine is aged in wood for only one year, and is therefore an early maturing wine, quite light on the palate in comparison to the heavyweights mentioned earlier.

Although Nebbiolo, in all these forms, is the most famous grape of Piedmont, it is certainly not the most common. That honour belongs to Barbera.

Barbera wines do not have to be made completely from Barbera grapes. To qualify for a DOC Barbera, a wine need only have 75 per cent Barbera, with up to 25 per cent coming from other grapes, such as Dolcetto and Freisa. An exception is Barbera di Monferrat, which must be 85 per cent Barbera and reach at least 12 per cent alcohol. Barbera d'Alba and Barbera d'Asti must be aged at least one year in the barrel and one more in the bottle. The latter is often considered to be the best of the Barberas.

Barbera wines are generally an intense garnet colour. In the mouth they are quite dry and acidic, often with a fair amount of tannin and, according to Hugh Johnson, some pluminess. They have a refreshing quality on the palate that makes them very suitable as an accompaniment to rich food.

But not all Piedmont wine is red. The famous bubbly, Asti Spumante, is a native to Piedmont as well.

Although "Asti Spumante" is its most common name, it can also be sold as Moscato d'Asti, Moscato d'Asti Spumante, or Moscato of any region producing the wine.

To qualify for DOC status, Asti Spumante must have a potential of 12 per cent alcohol by volume, but with only 7-9 per cent developed, so that some residual sugar is left unfermented. This residual sugar provides a certain sweetness in the finished wine that is important in enhancing the natural aroma of the Muscat grape from which the wine is produced.

Asti Spumante is made by the charmat method, which is distinguished by the fact that secondary fermentation takes place in large closed stainless steel tanks, before bottling. The advantage of this method is that the secondary fermentation takes place more quickly and therefore more cheaply than in the *méthode champenoise,* where secondary fermentation takes place slowly in the bottle. Italians claim, too, that the speed of the charmat method helps to preserve the distinctive aroma of the Muscat grape.

The aroma of Asti Spumante is compared by Sheldon Wasserman, author of *The Wines of Italy,* to "grapefruit, peaches, apricots or other ripe fruit." To me, it is not quite like any of these. It is Muscat. In the mouth, too, one notices the unusual flavour of the grape! However, it is fresh, sparkling and pleasantly sweet, making it a good companion to fruit dishes or desserts.

Tuscany

Tuscany is often described as the quintessence of Italy, the purest and proudest of all Italian regions.

Tuscan food follows suit, being noted for its simplicity and purity. Perhaps this stems from Etruscan history, with its somber spirit and aversion to excess.

Don't think for a moment, though, that simplicity and sobriety imply dullness or lack of quality. On the contrary, Tuscan food is famous for its excellence. It begins with top quality meat and produce, and prepares them with the kind of skill that you only see in Tuscany.

From Tuscany comes olive oil of international repute. In fact olives are often found growing in the same areas as the grapes of the region.

Tuscany's favourite pasta is rigatoni, not flat, as is common in the north, but tubular. However, flat ribbon-like varieties do exist.

Game is popular, as are stews and roasts. Beef is particularly popular, and in fact the most well known dish of the whole Tuscan region is *bistecca alla florentina,* basically a thick, tender T-bone steak cooked over an open fire. Simple, but delicious, it forms a perfect excuse for one of the region's great red wines.

Although Tuscany boasts many great wines, three stand out: Chianti Classico, Vino Nobile di Montepulciano, and Brunello di Montalcino.

Chianti

Chianti, the largest classified wine district in all of Italy, was upgraded in 1985 to the DOCG level. In typically Italian fashion, though, the region is segmented. In the early 1900s, powers in the heart of the Chianti area banded together to form a consortium whose aim it was to define and maintain quality standards for the area's wines. They called themselves the Chianti Classico consortium and adopted the symbol of a black rooster which is placed on the neck label of all its wines.

Producers outside this central core later decided that they, too, needed a consortium and a symbol. After all wasn't their wine just as good as that from the Classico area? So they formed the Putto consortium, and placed on wines meeting their regulations the symbol of a cherub, which is what "putto" means.

The wines of both consortia can be good wines. Most are best drunk young, while fruity and fresh. Riserva wine, however, is meant for keeping. It is aged for a minimum of three years in oak, and then is bottled after which it continues to improve for ten or more years. When mature a typical Chianti Riserva has a complex aroma with hints of oak, fruit and sometimes violets. On the palate it is dry, filling the mouth with the same complexities shown on the nose.

In recent history, two threads have woven together all Chianti wines. One is the grape blend, the other is the il governo technique used in the vinification of the wine. Both were established about 100 years ago by the Baron Ricasoli.

The blend of grapes permitted in Chianti is a perfect example of that typically Italian theme of "unity amidst diversity." The DOCG formula is: 50-80 per cent Sangiovese, 10-30 per cent Canaiolo, 5-10 per cent Trebbiano, 10 per cent Malvasia, and sometimes 5 per cent Colorino. This formula gives a lot of room for diversity of styles. Far from being haphazard though, each grape in this blend has a purpose: Sangiovese gives body and alcohol, Canaiolo gives aroma, Colorino provides colour, while Trebbiano and Malvasia both white grapes, serve to lighten the wine. In Chianti Classico the content of two white grapes drops to two to five per cent paving the way for wines of even deeper colour and fuller body.

The subject of "lightening" bring us to Ricasoli's second contribution to Chianti wines: the *il governo* technique. This refers to the practice of drying 5-10 per cent of a harvest on mats, then producing a very sweet must; then adding this sweet must to normally fermented wine. This induces a secondary (malo-lactic) fermentation, which helps to produce a fresh, lively wine.

The traditional Chianti flask, with its straw covering, was originally designed not for its looks but to preserve the wine's freshness by protecting it from the sun and preventing people from laying it on its side (it was rounded!) to age. Recent years, however, have seen the gradual demise of this flask. Cost is one reason, and marketing is another. Chianti producers would like the consumer to consider Chianti – especially the Riservas that are meant for ageing – as an alternative to Bordeaux. They are therefore using a Bordeaux type bottle especially for their longer lived wines.

Chianti today is in a state of change. The *governo* technique is on the decline, as newer vinification techniques are found to produce the same effects with less effort and risk. Recently pioneers like Antinori have been planting Cabernet Sauvignon and blending it with Sangiovese and Canaiolo to produce an excellent wine which he calls Tignanello. Full-bodied and complex it is a good accompaniment to the simple but full flavoured Tuscan food.

Vino Nobile

Vino di Montepulciano is made from a blend of grapes similar to that used for Chianti. Unlike Chianti, however they are vinified without the use of the *governo* technique. The vineyards lie in the commune of Montepulciano in the province of Siena.

The region's name is said to go back to the 17th century, when a poet by the name of Francesco Redi described the wine of Montepulciano as "the king of all wines." It has been called Vino Nobile di Montepulciano ever since. Like other areas of Tuscany, there are precise and detailed regulations governing its production and ageing.

The wine is dry and mildly tannic with medium body, and an aroma and flavour similar to a Chianti, as would be expected from its similar composition. Some claim that Vino Nobile has more finesse. In any case the wine is most enjoyable with simple meals.

Brunello

Geographically Montalcino is a part of the Chianti region; but in the world of wine it stands alone, for Montalcino is the home of Brunello.

According to Guglielano Solci, (Italian Wines and Spirits, July-Sept 1983), the name Brunello appeared for the first time in 1842 in a note written by a Montalcino priest – he was apparently praising the wine made from local Sangiovese grapes, which he described as 'brunello' because of its dark colour.

The Brunello wine that we know today was created in 1870 by Ferruccio Biondi-Santi. It is important to realize that this man was not the first to ever make a wine from the area's Sangiovese grapes – that had been done for decades.

What Ferruccio did was twofold. First he isolated and propogated a sub-variety of the Sangiovese – called the Sangiovese Grosso. Second, he vinified it without the traditional (and at that time unquestioned) *governo* technique. The wine thus borne was robust and strong, complex and truly different from other Chianti wines. It was called Brunello di Montalcino.

By keeping quality high and quantity low, the Biondi-Santi family was able to market Brunello as a "crème de la crème", an expensive, high status wine for the affluent. Awards at different competitions encouraged this image.

With time, others began producing Brunello di Montalcino. Today its quality and production is overseen by a local consortium which establishes and enforces detailed regulations concerning everything from grape yield to labelling practices.

The character of Brunello is best described by Burton Anderson (Vino - The Wines and Winemakers of Italy, p. 257), who calls it "tannic and high in alcohol, extract and acids, austere, warm, rich in body and colour and infinitely complex. If other wines could be described as big, Biondi-Santi's might be considered enormous."

It is marvellous with beef or lamb, especially roasts, or with game like partridge or duck. At the end of a meal, it would make an excellent accompaniment to Parmesan cheese.

THE WINE AND
FOOD OF RIOJA

A bottle of wine always tastes different after you have visited the region where it is produced. Or so I have found, after visiting the Rioja region of Spain. I went with the kind of preconceived idea that so often comes from limited experience – in this case, that all Rioja wines were heavy and woody, not something I loved. I returned a convert! Somehow, seeing the country, talking with its people, eating its food and reading its history really made a difference. It made me appreciate everything on a completely new level!

The Rioja district lies in the valley of the Ebro River, which flows from west to east across the northern portion of the country. The area has been subdivided into three subregions, each of which has its own climate and soil characteristics. The *Rioja Baja,* filling the eastern portion of the region, is relatively hot and dry. In comparison, the *Rioja Alta* (lying to the west, south of the Ebro) and the *Rioja Alavesa* (to the west also, but north of the river) receive less sunshine and more rain. The wines of the Baja are thus highly alcoholic and somewhat lacking in acidity, while those of the Alta and Alavesa possess more elegance and balance.

Much to my surprise, I learned that the winemaking methods in Rioja are largely the result of French influence! Apparently it had always been customary to ferment grapes in open stone vats, then transfer the new wine to large oak barrels for slow fermentation over the winter.

As early as the 1700s, Riojans were concerned with improving their wines. A native of Alavesa went to Bordeaux in order to study winemaking techniques, and came back telling everyone how the French were maturing their wines in oak. Although no one jumped at the news, producers began to look to France as a source of expertise.

In the 1860s French vineyards were invaded and ruined by phylloxera. But not so in Spain – at least, not yet. So French wine merchants poured into Rioja, which happened to be one of the closest places to go. Armed with experience and knowledge, they quickly became part of the local wine scene.

One vigneron from Bordeaux was hired by a wealthy Spanish nobleman, the Marqués de Riscal, to build a French style bodega. It was new and revolutionary, with all vessels constructed from oak. Two hundred and twenty-five litre barrels were used to age both the white and the red wines. This style of bodega became popular, and soon other Spanish aristocrats – with the help of Frenchmen – followed suit. Oak vats, and long ageing in Bordeaux type oak barrels (as the French had once done) became the norm.

When I asked one winemaker about the grapes used in Rioja, I was told that this was one thing the French did *not* bring! All major grapes used for Rioja wines are native to either Rioja itself or to some other region of Spain.

Four grapes dominate red Riojas. *Tempranillo* is an early ripening grape grown extensively in the Alavesa. The thick black skins of this grape contribute good colour to a wine. *Garnacha,* grown mostly in the Baja region, yields wine with a high alcohol content, and a tendency to oxidize easily to an orange colour. *Graciano* grapes contribute a pleasant aroma to the finished wine, while the *Mazuelo,* with their high tannin content, confer long life.

Each grape, it seems, has something special to offer, yet none is complete by itself! As each instrument in a symphony contributes to a harmonious blend of sounds, the grapes of Rioja blend together to produce well balanced wines.

Infinite variety is made possible by this blending! Each bodega takes some or all of the same grapes, but in differing proportions. Bodegas in the Alavesa tend to use a high proportion of Tempranillo – as much as 90 per cent. Bodegas in the Rioja Alta vary greatly in their blends. Muga uses 60 per cent Tempranillo in one of its wines, with Garnacha, Graciano and Mazuelo making up the rest. Lan uses 80 per cent Tempranillo for one of its blends, with Graciano and Mazuelo filling the remainder.

It is easy to see that Rioja wine cannot be described in a mere three words! All these different blends, coupled with the different climates and soils of the three subregions, and different amounts of ageing means that each new bottle of Rioja is a brand new taste adventure!

Tasting bears this out. Almost all Rioja wines I have tasted – both in Spain and at home – are robust and oaky. But the nuances are fascinatingly different from bottle to bottle. One has more acid, more elegance; another more fruit; another more oak, perhaps with a hint of vanilla. One is lighter and softer; another heavier and more robust. Most manage to combine fruit and oak in intriguing ways – influenced, perhaps, by the French, but in the end very Riojan, very delightful.

Perhaps the Riojan food contributes to this sense of delight, for any wine drunk alone runs the risk of tiring the palate. But add a complementary food, and the possibilities for pleasure are endless! Especially in Rioja, where the food and drink are so beautifully suited to each other.

Vegetables are the pride of Rioja. They grow in the region along the banks of the Ebro and Oja rivers. Asparagus, artichokes, beans, onions, potatoes, carrots – you name it, it's probably there. Fresh and succulent, the vegetables all have an intensity of taste that is truly a treat.

Imagine starting a meal with asparagus, tender and juicy, coated lightly with a dressing of olive oil and vinegar! An expensive treat in North America, this became commonplace during my visit to Rioja.

One evening in Logroño, a *menestra de legumbres,* or mixed vegetable stew, started the meal. Warm and hearty, it contained a variety of vegetables simmered in a light broth, with pieces of serrano ham providing a pleasant seasoning.

Fish and seafood often find their way into a Riojan meal. For in Spain even the most inland area is still not far from the sea. Squid, langoustines, shrimp, clams and other seafood are fresh and plentiful. So are freshwater fish – mullet, trout, sole and many others. And freshness is really the key. No matter how the fish is prepared, it almost has to taste good just because it is so fresh! But preparation does count. And the Riojans prepare fish in countless ways! Fried squid rings are common, just as in the south of Spain, and are usually served at the beginning of a meal. Cold boiled shrimp and langoustines are seen as well.

Mixtures of fish and seafood are often cooked together, usually stewed slowly with vegetables like pimentos and tomatoes. The result – a treat! Each piece of fish still has its own unique flavour, plus something more – something given by the harmonizing of flavours. And somehow it's all enhanced even further by a glass of white wine. White Riojas stand up well to these saucy fish stews. Their ageing in oak adds enough weight and complexity to the fruit to give them the ''umph'' that's needed.

On to the meat! Rioja contains a fair amount of dry upland area which supports neither vine nor vegetable. But sheep can graze easily. And so lamb is a speciality in the region.

The youngest ones – suckling lambs – are small and tender enough to be roasted whole, usually over an open fire. The meat, succulent and delicate, is complemented perfectly by the full-bodied fruitiness of a local red wine.

Lamb too old to be called suckling is often stewed. Riojans are fond of stews and seem to have a knack for putting the right things together. Perhaps it's because so much grows there. Or do the earthenware dishes, made out of Spain's own red clay soil, create a special flavour? Who knows! In any case, it's lovely to taste the harmonious blends that make up the local stews. One I tasted contained chunks of lamb in a sauce made of peppers and tomatoes, spiked with serrano and onions.

Poultry and game are also plentiful in Rioja. Although prepared in a multitude of ways, they are most often roasted or stewed.

Potatoes were the highlight of a meal served to me at a visit to Bodega Lan. Cooked "Rioja style", the dish was a delightfully tangy mixture of potatoes, onions, red peppers and chorizo sausage, all simmered together in a clear orange broth. The spice of the chorizo was well balanced by the smooth blandness of the potatoes. And so well suited to the red Reserva we drank with it!

Here was a perfect example of how the union of food and wine form something that's more than the sum of its parts. The spiciness of the food by itself would have become tiring quite quickly. Similarly the wine. In spite of its very aromatic bouquet and its full-bodied taste of fruit and oak, its effect would gradually diminish. Not because the wine is short – far from it, it's your taste buds that become saturated. But eaten and drunk together – like this potato dish with red Reserva – and the picture changes. One taste complements the other, each contributing a flavour that the other is lacking. The result is that both food and wine are special and exciting – right to the end.

Yes, Rioja is special – its wines, its foods, its people, its spirit – all inflenced, perhaps, by history, climate, soil and neighbours. The result is marvellously diverse, marvellously Riojan.

PART III

PUTTING
IT
ALL TOGETHER

NUTRITIOUS GASTRONOMY

*"It is a privilege of the human species to eat
without hunger and to drink without thirst."*
Jean Brillat-Savarin

Man eats for pleasure. He has learned to derive a certain good feeling from eating – a sensation that is strong enough to make him want to keep eating even after metabolic needs are met. In other words, the sensory properties of food often play a greater role than does its nutritional value.

This preoccupation with eating is hardly new. According to Jay Jacobs, the Greeks were quite good at it. In his book entitled "Gastronomy" he tells the most delightful story of how the ancient Greeks learned to use religion as an excuse for feasting.

"...it was an easy step for the Greeks to reverse altogether the ancient ritual of the sacrifice. This had begun with the ceremonial slaughter of a beast and its symbolic consumption by a god, which is to say, by fire. If the god in question happened to be a bit off his feed on a particular day and failed to consume the whole beast, well, what harm if mere mortals helped themselves to some leftover roast mutton? And since the Greeks had great respect but not much love for their gods, once they'd acquired a taste for godly viands it would have been a simple matter to dampen the appetites of their deities by stoking the sacrificial fire with a little less wood. And then progressively less, until one day the sacrificial sheep, ox, or whatever, instead of being scorched to the bone, came through its ordeal fit only for human consumption – that is, done to a turn."

The step from religious ritual to gastronomic pleasure was a simple one. In fact King Solomon is said to have "followed the ritual sacrifice of sheep and oxen with a modest little dinner party that didn't break up until 14 days after the guests – all male – had assembled." The Romans actually went so far as to make themselves sick!

The situation today may be less extreme than in Roman times, but not all that different.

For a lot of us, food represents a certain security. We learn right from infancy to associate food and love. We cry and food is given. Soon we feel better. This persists into adulthood! Food is reassuring. It doesn't talk back. It doesn't change. Food is one of life's nicest rewards. How can we not indulge? Furthermore, in everything from TV commercials to restaurants we're bombarded with sensory stimuli – we see food, we smell it, we anticipate it!

If we're taking someone out to dinner we feel compelled to order generously. After all, those unwritten rules have it that a guest takes his lead on how much to order from what his host orders. So the host orders everything, hungry or not. And how can he not finish it all? After all, he does have to pay for it! And from the guest's point of view: here's a free meal: take advantage of it.

There are many other reasons for eating (besides hunger). Some of us eat out of boredom; some out of tension; others because the TV is on. The list goes on and on, but the message is the same. Eating is very much a social and emotional event. The act of enjoying good food, for many of us, is totally distinct from the act of nourishing our body. After all, dosen't healthy eating mean cutting out all those foods we love best and getting into bran, yogurt and salads?

No! As a lover of good food (by nature), and a nutritionist (by profession), I intend to show that you can eat well – in both senses of the word.

Imagine a dinner featuring Duckling à l'Orange as the main course. Very French. Very gourmet. The ducklings are roasted to perfection, leaving their juicy flesh covered with a crisp, golden brown skin. Enhancing this is an orange flavoured sauce, easily prepared ahead. Peas and rice accompany the duckling, providing a contrast in both colour and texture. To drink, a bottle of your favourite red wine, perhaps a Côte Rôtie. For dessert, Poires Bordelaise. All in all, a mouthwatering example of "eating well."

Now let us examine the dinner from a nutritional point of view. In today's age of modern technology this is fairly easy to do. To facilitate patient consultations, I have recently developed a computer program which performs a detailed nutrient analysis on either a recipe or a person's daily food intake. Fast and easy, and handy for generating hard, cold facts about the food we eat!

As you now suspect, I put our imaginary duckling dinner through an analysis, allowing average food portions and three ounces of wine per person.

Each person at our imaginary dinner party consumed 1167 calories. Although this might be the total day's allotment for someone on a reducing diet, it is totally within reason for a normal active man or woman without weight problems.

Although exact energy requirements are very individual, an average active adult can maintain his or her weight on anywhere from 1800 to 3000 calories per day – depending, of course, on body size, age, activity level, and so on. In any case, 1167 calories for dinner is far from sinful.

You might be interested in knowing where the calories came from. The duck itself contributed 60 per cent, or 674 of the dinner's total calories, mainly due to its high fat content. The sauce contributed 98, the peas 55, the rice 92, the wine 80, and the dessert 168. These numbers should help dispel some common misconceptions. First, sauces are not necessarily fattening. Secondly, neither are starchy foods like rice, or alcoholic beverages like wine. Rather, it's the meat portions that we need to look at. If North Americans would only learn to cut down on their protein intake, the problems of obesity might dwindle considerably!

Most of us consume far too much protein in comparison to our needs. The recommended intake of protein for an average healthy adult is 44 grams per day for females and 61 grams per day for males. Our duck dinner gives each person about 46 grams of protein! Add this to what would probably be consumed at breakfast and lunch, and it's very easy to see that we eat too much protein. Not that this is dangerous, mind you. It's simply unnecessary, and expensive in terms of the caloric cost.

Wine, on the other hand, is a bargain! At 80 calories per three ounce glass, you can splurge and have a few; even a half bottle adds up to only 300 calories! This figure will, of course, vary somewhat according to the nature of the wine. The calories from wine come from its alcohol and its residual sugar. Therefore the sweeter the wine and/or the higher the alcohol content, the higher its caloric value. So a red wine is not necessarily "more fattening" than a white wine. If concerned about calories, concentrate not on colour, but content. Look for a dry wine with a low alcohol content. And watch what you eat! But you certainly need not feel guilty for drinking some wine, and certainly not for cooking with it, as cooking causes the alcohol to evaporate further reducing its caloric content.

Besides enjoyment there are possible health benefits to wine. Recent medical research has shown that in some people, a moderate intake of alcohol is correlated to reduced blood pressure and lowered incidence of cardiovascular disease.

There are also nutritional benefits. Wine often helps fight obesity. By promoting a more relaxed atmosphere and a slower pace of eating, wine often helps a person eat considerably less food, yet still derive a feeling of satisfaction from the meal.

It is often said that wine is a source of iron. It's true because a bottle of wine contains about three milligrams of iron. However, the recommended daily intake of iron is 14 milligrams for women under fifty (seven for women over fifty) and eight milligrams for men. That means a half bottle of wine per day could contribute from ten to twenty percent of the iron you require each day. Hardly in the same category as liver, but certainly worth counting. Besides, if you end your meal by finishing off that last glass of wine and therefore avoid drinking coffee, there is an added benefit. Research has shown that caffeine inhibits the absorption of iron. So replacing that end-of-the-meal coffee with wine not only gives you that extra bit of iron, it also prevents undesirable effects of caffeine.

We could go on and on, analyzing for all kinds of obscure vitamins and minerals. The point though, should now be clear. A gourmet meal is not nutritionally sinful – at least, it need not be, if handled with a little common sense.

Presenting a different viewpoint is a statement from William Beaumont, author of Experiments and Observations on the Gastric Juice and the Physiology of Digestion. "In the present state of civilized society, with the provocatives of the culinary art, and the incentives of highly seasoned food, brandy and wine, the temptations to excess in the indulgences of the table are rather too strong to be resisted by poor human nature."

It's surprising how many people share this view! Food to them is provocative and tempting, but something to be resisted, so they set up a self-imposed martyrdom, determined to "be good." Life becomes a bowl of lettuce. Self-denial becomes something to be proud of. "I'm really eating well," they boast. But for how long? The laws of physics say that anything unbalanced will fall. And so does this stoic way of eating. After a certain length of time on this denial routine the suppressed pleasure urge becomes so strong that it must be dealt with. And it is – by leaps and bounds. After all, you deserve it by now, don't you? You've been so good for so long! So the reward syndrome sets in and you indulge. But then you feel so guilty that you set in motion another cycle of the Sinful Stoic.

Forget about good and bad! There is no good and bad when it comes to eating. Food is not an emotional crutch. It is not a moral issue. It is not something to build character over. Eating is okay! Enjoying it is, too. Both eating and enjoying are a normal part of life – not a reward, not a security blanket, not a wicked indulgence, and not something for which you need permission from mother. That's right, food is a pleasurable and quite normal part of life.

But let me make one point absolutely clear. A healthy diet has absolutely nothing to do with the phrase "health food." It's true that many health foods are natural or organic or unprocessed. It's a fact that many of these health foods contain nutrients our bodies need. It's also a fact that many are potentially dangerous. For instance, herbal products may contain natural toxins or poisons;

unpasteurized honey is susceptible to the growth of dangerous bacterial spores. Even vitamins, organic or not (your body cannot distinguish between the two), may be harmful if taken in excess. So beware of "natural" – it may not be better. And remember the supermarket – it does contain most of the food you need to stay healthy. After all, brown rice is brown rice. Where you buy it makes little difference, except perhaps in price!

In all fairness, though, it must be mentioned that the supermarket also houses a lot of items that are high in fat, high in sugar, and low in nutrients. Knowledge of the health hazards of excess fat and sugar is growing; yet so is their consumption! Studies have shown that over the past 75 years, fat consumption has increased by about 25 per cent. The intake of simple sugars has increased by about 25 per cent as well, while the intake of potatoes, bread and grains has dropped. The reasons for these trends are numerous. From a technological point of view, sugar and fat contribute to longer shelf life and lower costs. From a sociological point of view, sugar and fat are equated with richness, affluence and, in general, acceptability. Unfortunately, the health point of view is somewhat more negative: excess sugar and fat consumption has been correlated with a number of diet-related disorders, including obesity, heart disease, tooth decay, and many others. In spite of the availability of sugar and fat, it is your responsibility to keep your intake to a moderate level!

This implies a certain amount of decision making on your own part. For instance, why not enjoy a piece of cake? Or some cream in a sauce? Or extra butter in cooking? Let's examine the caloric cost of these suggestions. A piece of cake will cost you about 500 calories; a quarter cup of cream, about 200 calories; a mere tablespoon of butter, about 110 calories.

These numbers should bring home an important point: namely, that the higher the fat content of a food, the greater its caloric value. This generalization, so easy to remember, can be extremely helpful. The moral of the story: make intelligent decisions about the food you eat (or drink). Weigh the cost (of calories) against the benefit (of enjoyment) and if the cost benefit ratio is favourable and or affordable, then go ahead and enjoy it. But do it consciously, not impulsively.

This is easier than it sounds. Remember our duckling dinner. Or consider a meal of Veal Marsala, served with buttered noodles, steamed green beans, and, of course, a glass of wine. Both contain many vitamins and minerals, a generous amount of protein, and a reasonable number of calories. I like to call it "nutritious gastronomy."

So what you eat can be surprisingly liberal, surprisingly gourmet. The catch lies in quantity. Most of us eat far too much of everything. Part of the reason is that we ignore many of the messages our body sends us. We are so busy tuning in to the sensory stimuli all around us, that we ignore our own internal cues!

What should you do? Learn to tune in to your body's hunger signals. Feed your body, not your mind. Eat when you're hungry – and stop when you're not. In that context, savour your food and enjoy it. As Thoreau once said, "He who distinguishes the true savour of his food can never be a glutton; he who does not cannot be otherwise."

Above all, keep in mind the concept of balance and moderation. Most of the foods you eat and enjoy every day are remarkably nutritious (or can be) in moderate quantities. Eat a variety of foods, keeping the level of fats and sugars reasonably low. Use wine to its best advantage, both in the glass and in the skillet and with each meal you eat, allow yourself a generous portion of pleasure and a liberal dose of responsibility. Happiness and health – what a wonderful combination!

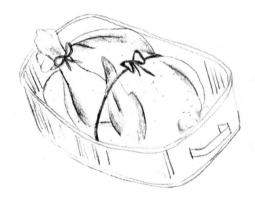

15

COOKING WITH WINE

Knowing the health benefits of wine drinking gives a wine lover one more excuse to enjoy a good bottle. In fact, any wine lover can tell you countless ways to enjoy wine: alone, with friends, at a tasting, before dinner, during dinner, after dinner...

A wine lover who loves to cook knows still another way to enjoy wine: in the kitchen. Here, wine takes on an entirely new dimension. Its colour, its acidity, and above all, its flavour mingle with other ingredients to create incredible taste combinations. Cooking with wine is the height of wine and food matchmaking, an excitingly creative way to unite food and wine and produce unparalleled marriages of flavour.

The idea is becoming more popular in North America. More and more people consider it "trendy" or "gourmet" to cook with wine. But why do so many people use Cuvée de Garbage for their cooking? When choosing a cooking wine, why do so many people say "it doesn't matter—it's only for cooking!"?

It *does* matter! Any dish coming out of the kitchen is only as good as its ingredients. You put garbage in—you get garbage out.

Besides, the cooking process often involves reducing the wine to intensify its flavour. If the wine was not very good to start with, think of what reduction will do! The flavour will go from bad to worse and detract from the appeal of the final product. But start with a pleasing wine and the result can be magnificent. A word of caution, though; wines that are very dry, delicate – no matter how pleasant to drink – are often not the best candidates for cooking, as they tend to lose their flavour in the process.

Does that mean you use your 1973 Château Léoville LasCases next time you cook a Bordelaise sauce? I hope not! That would be somewhat extravagant – akin to using your mahogany dining room table for firewood.

Drinking a well-aged wine can be an incredible and sensual experience. Volatile esters and acids bombard the nose, carrying fragrant and complex aromas. In the mouth, taste and aroma mingle with the the subtleties of fruit and wood providing a fantastic sense of enjoyment. All dependent on those volatile organic compounds attacking your sensory receptors!

Boil off those compounds in a saucepan and all this delight is lost into the air. What a waste! But take a young wine, full of fruit, but still tannic, and filled with non-volatile compounds, and the story changes. Now cooking enhances the wine, softening the tannins and bringing out the fruitiness.

With the old versus young question answered, you may still wonder about what wine to choose for what recipe. There are, of course, the traditional combinations. Choose red wine with red meats and white wine with white meats and fish. Pick dry wines with a main course and sweet wines with dessert.

Many people – and books – sadly stop there. There are so many unconventional combinations that are so absolutely wonderful. For instance, if you take a look at international gastronomy, you find dishes like Coq au Chambertin, Veal with Marsala, Poulet au Champagne, Kidneys in Sherry, Fish Stew with Rosé...the list goes on and on.

One principle that emerges from this tour is that regional dishes usually marry well with regional wines. The reason why? Some experts say it has to do with the fact that the grape vines and the food have grown in similar soil, and have absorbed similar minerals and nutrients – thereby producing a taste compatibility.

Although this may be true, I tend to put my trust in the natural culinary instincts of generations of ordinary men and women. For most, recipes date back to mothers and grandmothers, who had no access to international trade or exotic foods flown in by jet. Ingredients for recipes tended to come from one's own backyard or from what was available in the local village. That applied to both food and wine. Thus a dash of economics was blended with a pinch of personality and a liberal amount of culinary genius to produce an incredible recipe called Local Cuisine.

In Provence, for example a local rosé was added to the fisherman's pot along with the day's catch. In Burgundy, some tough old beef or poultry was stewed in local wine until flavourful and tender. Far away in Jerez de la Frontera, people were doing the same thing – using wine to add flavour to a food. Only here, they used what they had available, namely sherry. And so were born dishes like Chicken in Sherry, Kidneys in Sherry, and many more. Ordinary people all over the world were doing "what came naturally" – with marvellous results. A good lesson!

In general, you can create all sorts of interesting combinations and they'll be successful as long as you remember the concept of *balance*.

That means that neither wine nor food should be overwhelming. Each is meant to enhance the other, not mask one another. Thus a strongly flavoured wine blends well with a strongly flavoured food, but overpowers a milder food. Similarly, a delicate wine would make a definite contribution to a cream sauce for fish, but would get completely lost in a more intense beef-based sauce such as Bordelaise.

Remember everything is relative. Your perception of both food and wine can change, depending on the situation in which you place them.

This applies to both the table and the kitchen. If adding wine to a recipe, make sure it serves a purpose and adds a suitable flavour to the final dish. It should neither overpower nor get lost. For example, a light bodied white wine would show up nicely in a sauce over a delicate fish such as Dover Sole, but would seem insipid and weak in a Sicilian fish stew, where the flavours of both fish and garnishes are rather assertive. So choose carefully, and don't ruin a marvellous wine by putting it in the wrong company.

Speaking of the wrong company...I remember cooking my first wine sauce. It was going to be a white wine sauce for fish. Butter was melted, flour added to form a roux –big time cooking! To the roux I needed to add both white wine and milk. I opened the Muscadet, took out my large measuring cup and poured ½ cup of wine into it. Now I needed 1½ cups of milk or cream. Why make dishes dirty for nothing? I poured the milk into the same measuring cup as the wine. Instant flop! Forget about saving on dishes. Wine and milk were obviously not meant to be that intimate.

I later learned that the acidity of the wine affected the proteins in the milk and caused them to shrivel into a curdled mess. To prevent this from happening, the wine should be added to the roux by itself and stirred to form a very thick mixture. Then the milk or cream can be incorporated, and cooking continued to finish the sauce.

Another pearl of wisdom from the world of science: acids tend to reduce the thickening power of starches. So when making a wine sauce, you may find that you need to increase the amount of flour or whatever thickener you normally use. Or, decide on a thinner sauce. Remember, excess thickness may be great for glue, but it is not always an asset for sauces.

In many sauce recipes, the wine must be "reduced." This is a technique which is neither mysterious nor difficult. Reduction is, in a nutshell, evaporation.

The wine is poured into a saucepan or frypan. I prefer the latter, because its larger surface area makes the work go faster. On goes the heat – to as high as possible. Leave the pan uncovered and wait. But watch! It goes faster than you think. So don't go yakking on the phone or your wine is liable to dry up and burn.

For how long do you let it boil? That depends on the recipe. Often recipes will say "...until reduced to half its original volume." That means if you started with two cups of wine, let it boil for a few minutes, then pour the wine from the pan to a nearby measuring cup. If it measures more than one cup, it still needs more boiling. If it measures less, you've gone too far! Similarly, a recipe that states "until reduced by one third" means that if you start with one cup of wine, you boil it down until it measures two thirds of a cup. And so on: the mathematics is often the most difficult part.

Now that you know how to do it, you may wonder why the whole thing is necessary. The answer lies in flavour. A major reason for adding wine to a recipe in the first place is its flavour. Being a beverage, wine has a large amount of water. In fact, it is almost eighty per cent water! Reducing the wine gets rid of much of this water, thereby concentrating the flavour of the wine. That means you get the benefit of lots of flavour without dilution.

During the reduction process, the alcohol content of the wine evaporates. A shame, you say? Definitely not! The presence of alcohol in the finished dish usually results in a harsh, burning taste – distinctly undesirable. Getting rid of the alcohol helps to mellow the taste of your food and improve its mouthfeel. It's also good news for diabetics and anyone else advised to avoid alcohol: as long as it's cooked, it's okay to enjoy the flavour guilt-free.

Using wine in a sauce imparts flavour in a fairly direct manner: the wine is an integral part of the finished product. However you need not be a sauce expert to enjoy wine in cooking. There are other ways! For instance, you can marinate meat, poach fish, stew fruits, or even freeze the wine to make a sherbet. In all cases, the wine plays an important role. Like love, it seems to bring out the best in everything around it!

It's true! And furthermore, there's a reason why. It all has to do with those two magic properties of wine: flavour and acidity. In a marinade, the wine diffuses into the meat, giving the meat some of its flavour. At the same time, the acidity of the wine helps to break down the tough fibres of the meat, helping to make it more tender. The choice of wine in marinating is governed by the same principles discussed earlier for food in general. Don't use your 1961 Latour, but don't use stuff you hate either. Don't overwhelm. Remember the concept of balance. Remember the role of acidity, and choose a wine with lots of it.

And in this case, remember colour as well. A red wine with deep colour and lots of tannin will impart a deep colour to the finished dish. For example, some Zinfandels, Barberas and Burgundies will do this. On the other hand, a white wine will usually not affect a meat's colour at all. However, the high acidity of many white wines makes them perfect for tenderizing and flavouring meats like veal, pork and rabbit.

What do you do with all this marinade after the meat has finished soaking? You might want to use it to baste the meat while it's cooking. For instance, after marinating beef cubes in a red wine marinade, you can put the meat on skewers and broil them. Basting the meat during broiling will help enhance both its colour and flavour. In another situation, you might want to cook the meat right in its marinade! An Alsatian recipe for rabbit in Riesling does this. A marinade is made from a good Alsatian Riesling, which, by the way, makes a beautiful marinade because of its high acidity and gorgeous fruitiness. Then the meat is stewed in the marinade until tender, all the while absorbing its flavour. Finally, the liquid is reduced and cream added to form a sauce. The wine plays a key role from start to finish! Can you see why the quality of wine is important?

Although cooking food in a wine-containing marinade sounds attractive, you should realize that it is not always necessary. You can poach or stew a food in wine without marinating it first! An interesting example is *Pears poached in Red Wine* – an unlikely, but fabulous combination. Or look at chicken. In Champagne, they have *Poulet au Champagne*; in Burgundy, they have *Coq au Chambertin*; in Alsace, they have *Coq au Riesling*. And how about fish? The famous *Bouillabaisse* of Provence is really only a collection of fish stewed in wine! But what a stew! And poached salmon – so sought after in North America – is usually cooked in a *court bouillon* containing wine.

The case of poaching fish is particularly interesting. Fish sold in any inland city is never truly fresh – at least not as fresh as fish right out of the water. Often not-so-fresh fish have strong, "fishy" odours caused by the presence of chemical compounds called "amines." Highly volatile, these amine-containing molecules jump up at you, offending your nose and also your palate. The solution: get rid of them! How? Anything acidic. Yes, anything acidic will react chemically with any amines in the fish and render them impotent. So choose vinegar or lemon juice to cook your fish – if you like the taste of vinegar or lemon juice. Or choose wine: it's both acidic and pleasant tasting. It will tie up any foul smelling amines, and at the same time, provide a moist medium in which the fish can cook, allow its flavour to permeate the flesh of the fish, and yield an absolutely delightful marriage of food and wine.

You might be thinking by now that cooking with wine commits you to hours in the kitchen – marinating, slow stewing and poaching, complicated sauce making, and so on. Not true! Wine can be used to good advantage in conjunction with quickly sautéed dishes. In this situation, the meat is sautéed, then removed from the pan. Invariably, there are rich, delicious tasting residues left, possibly along with the remaining fat. Stop! Don't wash that pot! Pour off the fat, then "clean" ("deglaze") the pan with a splash of wine. That's right! Turn the heat to high, pour in the wine, and scrape with a wooden spoon while the wine boils and retrieves the rich-tasting remains left from the meat. Finish with a dab of butter, let the boiling continue until the desired taste intensity is reached, and voilà – a gourmet dish in less than five minutes. And this technique can be used for any sautéed meat, in combination with any one of many different wines. One of my favourite examples of this technique is *Veal Marsala*.

Actually, I have a lot of favourites in the kitchen. For me cooking is a truly satisfying experience. The satisfaction comes from being able to understand some basic principles, then use them to turn delectible dreams into lucious realities.

Menu Planning

Although a knowledge of cooking techniques will enable you to create a wide variety of fabulous dishes, it is not always enough to ensure a top-notch dinner party. At the heart of every successful dinner is a well planned menu. In fact it is the most essential ingredient of the evening and, like most things, is the result of careful thinking based on both science and art.

Planning a menu is like writing a story or building a house. You must know the individual components or building blocks, then understand how to put them together to make sense and say something meaningful. This is the real skill, representing the creative application of sound knowledge. Use the concepts discussed earlier in this book, adaptation, relativity and the effect of order, to produce the dinner of your dreams.

The principle of adaptation, you will recall, refers to the condition whereby you get used to a taste or aroma and "lose" your ability to perceive it. Too much of the same thing, even a good thing, gets boring. However, change combats boredom. This has a number of practical implications with regard to menu planning:

• Firstly, it means that no food should appear twice in a row on one menu, even if prepared in different ways. For example, if you feature Cream of Carrot Soup as a first course, then you should avoid serving Carrot Coins as a vegetable with the main course. Or, if Asparagus in Puff Pastry is served as a first course, then Beef Wellington would not be your main course. To a certain extent, this applies to wine as well. Assuming that you are serving a multi course dinner, it would be boring to serve the same wine with all courses. An interesting exception would be if you are planning a theme event; let's say "the many faces of Chardonnay." In that case, it might be interesting to feature a seafood appetizer with a Chablis, followed by a main course fish with Meursault, then a dessert accompanied by a Chardonnay-based bubbly.

- Colours as well should be alternated, both between and within the courses. To understand the importance of this, imagine a dinner that starts with Vichyssoise, followed by Creamed Chicken with Cauliflower and Boiled Potatoes, then vanilla ice cream for dessert! Boring is hardly the word. But don't be fooled; on a less extreme scale, it's easy to fall into this trap by serving something like fish in a cheese sauce, then chicken in a cream sauce. With wine this rule doesn't apply: to constantly alternate between white and red would violate the principles of relativity and order, as you will see shortly.

- That brings us to garnishes. They too should be varied, which means if you garnish a pâté dish with cherry tomatoes, use something else for the main course. In addition, avoid serving everything with rich sauces. Even the French don't do that!

- Texture and shape should also be interesting. So unless you are catering to the local "over ninety" crowd, make sure your dinner features crunchy foods as well as soft, and chewy as well as smooth. The shape of the foods needs to be varied too, so that visual stimuli are exciting.

- Cooking methods should not repeat themselves in a menu, at least not obviously. For example, if poached fish is a first course, then avoid something like boiled chicken as the next course. If the menu is long, with many different courses, it is often necessary to repeat a technique: this is no problem as long as there is at least one different method separating the two similar ones.

All we are really talking about here is variation which is quite simple, actually though not enough in itself.

On a more practical and very necessary level, are matters like cost and availability of the food and wine you are serving. What are the likes and dislikes of your guests? Are you going to plan the food around the wine, or the wine around the food? Look over your menu and its recipes. Do you have all the equipment needed and more importantly, the skills? How much needs to be done at the last minute? Will you be harried by the pressure of your guests being there? Always choose a menu that will enable you to enjoy your own party!

The other important principle is relativity and the effect of order. In a nutshell, this means that anything you eat or drink is perceived in light of what has just preceded it. No matter how interesting or how varied your menu, always consider this idea of order.

In terms of food, it means never begin a meal with a strong spicy dish because everything after it will seem bland and tasteless. In addition, avoid serving sweet dishes at the start of a meal; it will make the food following it seem somewhat bitter. In general, it's best to start off with something mild and let the flavours build as the meal progresses.

The progression of wine follows similar principles all narrowing down to the idea that what you think of a wine depends largely on what has come before. If you remember this, it makes sense that you should serve:
* delicate before assertive
* young before old
* light before full-bodied
* dry before sweet
* less complex before more complex
* whites before reds
* less important before more important

These are generalizations, not hard and fast rules. When matching food and wine in a dinner situation, it's often impossible to follow absolutely every rule to the letter. Don't worry, rules are only goals to strive for and are not meant to be taken too seriously. What is most important is common sense. Always remember what goes before and after a particular wine. No wine should be over-powered by what preceded it; nor should it ruin what is to come.

If a wine is used in the cooking of a particular dish, you should consider serving the same type of wine (but perhaps of better quality) to drink with it. If a menu features food from a particular country, it's a good idea to build your progression of wines around that country as well.

This brings us to another important point. A good menu needs to have a central idea, or theme, to hold it all together. A theme could be based on wine, or food, on the season, or on a country or region of the world. For example, every November brings the Beaujolais Nouveau, a perfect excuse for wine lovers to get together. Plan some nibbles that suit the wine and voilà, an evening of fun. You might be planning an after-ski get-together where a cheese fondue and Swiss Neufchâtel would be easy and appropriate. Other seasons might bring other ideas. Perhaps "An evening in Spain"; or "a tour of Canada."

Being a wine lover, you might base an evening on the wines of a particular country; you would choose the wines you want to feature first, then plan the food around the wine. In some cases, you may even build a dinner around one particular bottle of wine. Perhaps a very special bottle. You may have only the one bottle, maybe you won it in a winetasting competition, or maybe you brought it back from your last wine tour. You have been waiting so long for just the right opportunity to serve it.

Is this you? If so, you are setting yourself up for disaster. That special bottle might or might not stand up to the glorious ideas in your head. For one thing, wines vary from bottle to bottle. Older wines are particularly prone to bottle differences.

Secondly, your emotional state and your mood are constantly changing. This is important, because how you feel, who else is present, the general atmosphere, all affect your perceptions of both food and wine. The wine that tasted so delightful in the grower's cellar in France might not be quite the same back home in the real world.

Thirdly, remember that wines tasted alone at a tasting (with no food) always leave you with different impressions that when foods are present. It's not necessarily a case of better or worse, it's just different. So don't be disappointed if the wine to which you gave five stars out of five at a tasting seeme not quite right at dinner.

With all these variables playing on your memory, it's no wonder that your special bottle has a question mark above its halo. If only there were some way to be more sure and to know that your great wine will be at its best when that moment comes.

There is a way. It's called a "sacrificial lamb." To understand this concept, imagine yourself tasting some of the first growths: let's say Château Lafite, Château Latour, and Château Margaux. In spite of their fame, it's very likely that you will find yourself saying "ho hum" to at least one of them. I remember being at a first growth tasting where twelve out of fifteen people actually refused a glass of Lafite. A shame, but next to the others, it was just another first growth, not the most preferred of the evening. However, that same lafite, put in a tasting with some unclassified châteaux, would shine like the brightest star. It's all in the company one keeps . . .

You should see the idea of relativity coming back again. What you taste now conditions your palate and sets up your taste buds for what you taste next. How you perceive that great wine, therefore, depends on what you have just tasted before it. If it was another "great" wine, you risk being disappointed with your "star bottle." What you need before that special bottle is a sacrificial lamb, something that is similar but purposefully younger or more mediocre. As I have said before, it's all a set-up. You are making relativity and the effect of order work to your advantage.

Try it at your next dinner party. Whether you have a first course with wine or not, consider having a glass of a minor and younger wine of the same or similar appellation as the great wine you intend to serve as the main feature of your meal. Make no mention of this to your guests until you are ready to serve the second (special) wine. The first glass will have conditioned their palates, serving as a pleasant, but easy act to follow. Disappointments will be a thing of the past. That special bottle will shine in all its glory.

Really, all you have done is planned. You have used the idea of relativity and order, planting that "sacrificial lamb" in order to have all the lights shine on that one special bottle. That bottle becomes the focal point of your evening.

It's important to have a focal point in an evening; even the best theme needs something to focus on – a highlight, so to speak. Everything builds up to it, then gradually winds doem from it. Sometimes the focal point is that famous wine bottle; other times, it's a food: Beef Bordelaise, or perhaps Duckling with Port Sauce. Most often, it's the combination of food and wine at a particular point in the evening that becomes the moment of glorious pleasure that your guests will always remember. For good reason, too. You planned it that way!

Trip to the south of France

Pissaladière
Lirac

Bouillabaisse
Tavel
Sauce Rouille
French Bread

Green Salad

Tarte au Fromage
Sauternes

Bouillabaisse is one of those things that by its very nature demands a crowd. Being a fisherman's stew, it requires that the catch of the day be thrown into the pot, and the catch of the day always involves a bit of everything. So you can see that making bouillabaisse for two is somewhat difficult unless your "bits of everything" are microscopic.

Bouillabaisse needs people for another reason. It's fun to eat and what a shame not to share that fun with friends. There's that piece of lobster to attack, a shrimp that needs peeling, a mussel to extract from its shell, perhaps a chunk of lotte to spear...then of course, there's the broth itself. An evening full of informal fun and for seafood lovers, a real treat.

Choosing wine for Bouillabaisse is difficult. On one hand you need a wine compatible with seafood, so Chardonnay or Muscadet, something fairly light with a crisp acidity, might come to mind. But wait! Bouillabaisse is more than just fish and seafood. As a typical Southern French dish, it contains a generous amount of garlic and tomato. The dish is definitely assertive, rather than light and delicate. It can easily squelch any Chardonnay or Muscadet. What to do? Think regional. Think rosé. Tavel in particular would have enough strength to match the assertiveness of the Bouillabaisse, yet still refresh the palate. Yes, the Tavel and Bouillabaisse will be the stars of this show, supported by the traditional Sauce Rouillé and some good French bread. Both the Bouillabaisse and its accompanying sauce can be cooked ahead of time, and rewarmed gently. In fact, they actually benefit from this timing which better allows the flavours to blend.

For an introduction, we need something to set the stage and attune the palate. Staying with a Provençal theme, we could select a Pissaladière, prepared ahead, then baked just before serving. Its combination of tomatoes, anchovies, olives and onions excite the senses and pave the way for what's to come.

The wine to go with this should stand up to the flavour of the Pissaladière, yet not be too dominant. Remember that we have planned for the Tavel to be the featured wine of the evening. Although somewhat unconventional, I would suggest a light red, such as a Lirac. It is relatively fruity, not too serious and a good meal starter.

Now that the beginning is set, we need to consider the end. After that strongly flavoured main course, we need to lead down, cleansing the palate and making way for dessert. It would be an injustice to jump from the garlic, tomato and fish straight to dessert. Their aftertaste would distort and detract from most sweets. A simple green salad is a perfect solution. Its crunch and acidity provide a refreshing change from what has preceded and form a pleasant way to begin our "dénouement."

But even with that, a dessert needs careful thought. The meal up until now has been delectable, but certainly not delicate. So why start now? Let's go strong, instead, and use a Tarte au Fromage served with a Sauternes. The tart uses a puff pastry base, with a topping of Gorgonzola, Boursin and whipped cream. It's forward, which is what you need to end a meal like this, yet complex and different enough to keep you wanting just one more bite. The Sauternes has the acidity and the richness, along with that botrycized taste, to stand up to both the tart that accompanies it, and the main course that preceded it. So in both the wine and the food, we have maintained a constant intensity of taste, yet at the same time we built and progressed to form a most memorable meal – a gastronomic trip to the south of France.

An Italian Feast

Breadsticks wrapped
with Prosciutto
Asti Spumante

Minestrone

Eggplant Parmesan
Pinot Grigio
Friuli

Veal Cacciatore
Buttered Pasta
Valpolicella

Spinach Salad

Italian Cheese/Fruit
Brunello

Italian meals are like rolling hills – they go on and on and on, forming a seemingly endless succession of dishes, each following naturally from the one that came before and leading gently into its successor. There is no main course in the sense that North Americans use the word. At no time are you served a large quantity of one food, along with three or four "side dishes." Instead you see a progression of small portions in harmony with each other and reflecting the season's bounty. Vegetables are used often, yet in different forms, for variety and freshness are essential components in any Italian meal.

Our menu begins with breadsticks rolled in prosciutto. About half the length of each breadstick is wrapped in a piece of thinly sliced prosciutto, so that each stick is partially covered and partially exposed. Easy to prepare and easy to eat standing up, it provides a crunchy and stimulating start to any evening. A wine accompanying this needs to stand up to the salty-sweet taste of the ham, yet leave room for other stars to shine later. A light, dry bubbly from the Asti region would be suitable.

At the table, we are introduced to heartier fare. A minestrone soup is a wonderful way to use fresh vegetables and herbs and is a favourite Italian meal starter. It can be prepared a day or two ahead and simply rewarmed before serving. In fact, it's much like great wines: it improves with age – days though, not years! This soup stands alone with no wine required.

Eggplant Parmesan (another do ahead dish) is a natural sequel to the soup in that it uses a vegetable as its main ingredient. This time it's in the form of a casserole, moistened with tomato sauce and topped with a generous amount of fontina and mozzarella. These two cheeses are mild, yet distinct in their taste. The fontina especially, has that earthy, truffly taste that is uniquely Piedmont. Because of the predominance of cheese in this dish, it dictates our choice of wine, in this case, a white wine such as Pinot Grigio from Friuli, or Soave or Verdicchio. The crisp lightness of these wines is necessary to refresh the palate between the smooth, rich mouthfuls of cheese.

Next comes the meat and the pasta. As is typical in Northern Italy, the meat is veal. It is sautéed quickly, bathed in a tomato sauce laced with Marsala, and smothered with vegetables. Buttered noodles provide an effective support for the veal, counterbalancing the latter's complexity with their own simplicity. The wine to drink with this course needs to be fairly light in body, like the veal, with enough acidity to be lively and just enough character to be interesting. A Valpolicella would fit the bill.

After the meat course in most Italian menus comes a vegetable or salad. An abundance of cooked vegetables has already been offered, so a salad would be nice at this point. Why not make use of spinach, but with a difference? Add a fruit and use the salad as a bridge toward dessert. My favourite combination is spinach, red peppers and lychees; not Italian, to be sure, but absolutely astounding. All by itself – no wine, thank you; at least not until the salad is finished and the cheese and fruit are served.

Your platter might include Gorgonzola, Parmigiano-regiano (solid, not grated) and a medium or mild Provolone, along with fresh fruits of the season. For a wine, you need to build on the progression you have already started. The last wine (with the main course) was a Valpollicella – light and fairly simple, well suited to the veal it accompanied. Furthermore, it acted (unknowingly at the time) as a perfect wine to set up your last wine of the evening; a mature Brunello, dry, full-bodied and full of complexities, it stands majestically alongside the cheese and fruit as the focal point and a fitting end to that dazzling succession of dishes you have just called dinner.

Chablis for Dinner

Cheddar Crisps
Vinho Verde

Carrot Vichyssoise

Lobster in White Wine Sauce
Chablis Grand Cru
Mellow Yellow Rice
Spinach with Pine Nuts

Green Salad
Cheese and Fruit
Port

The sun is setting while a warm summer breeze whispers its way through the trees and bushes. You're tasting a 1978 Grand Cru Chablis: it's austere, yet elegant; flinty, yet fruity; dry and crisp. A harmonious state of pleasure and serenity envelops you. If only you could make this moment last forever . . .

Suddenly an idea: make it happen again! Plan a dinner evening with old friends focusing on your Chablis. Think back to the concepts discussed earlier in this book.

If chosen carefully, food will heighten your enjoyment of the Chablis. To honour and enhance the wine, the food must be elegant and important, yet subtle enough to support rather than dominate.

Fish or seafood comes to mind. But what? Broiled halibut? Too plain. Bouillabaisse? Important enough, but too strongly flavoured – it would overpower the wine. Broiled lobster? Getting closer: the fleshy saltiness of the shellfish would go well with the crisp flinty fruitiness of the Chablis. But boiled lobster is somewhat too casual. How about dressing it up? Yes, that would be just right. Steam the lobster for a short time, remove the meat and combine it with a creamy sauce. The sauce could contain some Chablis, forming an intimate relationship between the food and the wine. Stuff the mixture back into the shell, and voilà: an elegant and important lobster dish, the perfect marriage of wine and food. Neither will overwhelm the other. Rather, each will supplement its partner: the wine, dry and crisp, steely, yet fruity; the lobster, fleshy and delicate, bathed in a creamy essence of the wine itself.

To accompany this great combination, you need a contrast in colour and texture, a different taste but not overpowering. Spinach sautéed with pine nuts adds colour and crunch, with a mild nutty flavour. Rice would round out the place, but by itself is too white. Add a pinch of tumeric and you have a colourful addition to the plate; mellow yellow rice.

That's the main course – the focal point of the dinner, the climax of the evening. Now the before and after.

Important things first. You need a wine to serve before dinner. It should be less important than the Chablis, so that by comparison the Chablis will look great (which is what you want!). The before dinner wine should be light and lively, stimulating to the palate. How about a dry white Vinho Verde with its lively pétillance, it's clean youthful taste made interesting by a hint of wood and spice? Yes, that would be lovely. And to munch with it? Cheddar Crisps would go well. Served warm, they are crunchy and crisp, with a Cheddar aroma that is sure to waken the senses and stimulate the appetite.

Now to the table. A smooth, mild tasting soup would be a welcome contrast after the tangy Cheddar, and would clean the mouth in preparation for the main course. A carrot Vichyssoise, served cold, would fit the bill. Unusual and interesting, this pale orange soup can stand alone with pride. No wine is needed. The soft, smooth thickness of the carrots and cream is enough and is a marvellous introduction to the Chablis and lobster which form the main course.

Now the dénouement – the winding down. A salad is a good sequel to the main course. Crisp and cool vegetables are moistened with an herbed vinaigrette. Strong in flavour, strong in acidity it is refreshing and cleansing. No wine is wanted here: the acidity of the salad dressing would distort and ruin the taste of any wine. But do not worry – the salad refreshes the palate and prepares the mouth for the next course.

Something smooth-textured would be nice after the salad; something flavourful, yet not too strong.

Fancy, French and Formal

Cheese Straws
Champagne

Smoked Salmon Plate
Tokay d'Alsace

Steak Chasseur
Molded Potatoes
Parsleyed Carrots
Young AC Burgundy
then
Mature good quality
Côte de Nuits

Cheese/Fruit

Crèpes Suzette
Grand Marnier

I am not sure what it is exactly that gives French cooking its mystique. Perhaps the same thing that gives French wines their fame and repute. Centuries of history and local know how and that perfect mix of science and creative genius. Whatever it is, a French menu is always popular with dinner guests and easier to prepare than you think.

In planning a French menu, it's especially important to think carefully of what wines you want to feature. Because there are so many incredible wines to choose from, it is very tempting to want to feature all the "greats" in one meal.

Many wine experts agree that if you feature more than one "really great" wine at a meal you are looking for trouble. One will fight with the other, splitting the vote. With only one "great" running, though, it is a clear victory. So you need to pick your leader. All the other wines, and the foods, will be planned around it.   As an example, let us suppose that you want to show off a high quality Burgundy, let's say a Chambertin from Côte de Nuits. Its full body and complex Pinot Noir character demand a substantial and important food, yet one which will support the wine rather than detract from it. Beef is a traditional accompaniment to Burgundy. But plain beef is boring. Let's use individual filets and dress them up. A Sauce Chasseur, fitting, in that its mushrooms give it an "earthy" quality that forms a kind of taste bridge between the wine and the beef. To round things out and add some colour, we can try Parsley Carrots and Molded Potatoes. The latter is similar to scalloped potatoes, but baked in small molds, then turned out to form extremely pretty and important looking portions.

All this is too important to spoil with disappointment. We need to give ourselves the assurance that the wine (and the food) will be as perfect as possible. The food is no problem. The sauce is made ahead of time, and the beef is easy to prepare at the last moment. The potatoes and the carrots are assembled ahead and cooked with little effort before serving. The wine is what needs some setting up in the form of a "sacrificial lamb." As we discussed earlier, a sacrificial lamb is similar to the important wine, but more mediocre. It sets the stage by giving the palate an easy act to follow. In this case, a young A.C. Burgundy would do beautifully. Only a small glass of it is necessary, served while you are bringing the main course to the table. This glass also enables you to be more relaxed while you serve the main course, as you have the assurance that your guests are quite happy, sitting and sipping. Don't explain all this philosophy – just follow it!

Then when you bring the main course to the table and pour that special bottle of Chambertin, you will know that everything is going to be perfect. Your guests will rave, both about the food and the wine.

With the main event so well planned, it's time to look at the kind of introduction you want to give it. In this case, the main course will involve a certain amount of last minute attention. It would make life easier, then, to have a first course that requires no last minute preparation or heating. Something cold will fulfil these requirements and also add variety to the menu.

As guests arrive, you can serve Cheese Straws with a light style bubbly, be it Champagne or other. The Cheese Straws are fingers of pastry dough, coated with cheese and paprika, then baked (ahead of time) until puffy and light. Delicate, but rich, they form a perfect foil for the bubbly and give the evening an elegant beginning.

A smoked salmon plate carries this elegance to the table. The best quality smoked salmon you can get is placed on a bed of greens and topped with a wedge of lemon, some diced Spanish onion, capers, minced parsley and a triangle or two of pumpernickel bread. It is all put on individual plates hafead of time to avoid unnecessary work at the last minute. Placed on the dinner table just before your guests sit down, these plates form a tantalizing welcome to the meal. With it, a well chilled Tokay d'Alsace would be suitable, with its crisp richness and hint of smoke bringing out the best in the food.

That brings us back to the main course again, ready to wind down. Cheese and fruit is a nice way to finish our wine and lead toward a dessert course. The assortment of cheeses should take into consideration the wine to be finished: in this case, Chambertin. That means strongly flavoured cheeses. At least one should be blue (pick your favourite), with other possibilities being Havarti and/or a medium Gouda. For fruit accompaniments you usually need to rely on what is in season.

If the cheese and fruit were to end the meal, then something like Port could carry your guests on for the rest of the evening. If you want to go all out, though, add a dessert to the menu. What is more spectacular then Crêpes Suzettes? Yes, you can do it! The crêpes are made ahead. The sauce is either made at the table (if you are that type) or, if you prefer, made completely in advance and reheated in a skillet with the crêpes. It is guaranteed to be as good or better than you would get at an expensive restaurant. Served with Grand Marnier, it is an impressive end to a truly great dinner.

PART IV

A COLLECTION
OF
ORIGINAL RECIPES

CHEDDAR CRISPS

4 oz. (125 g) butter (room temperature)
4 oz. (125 g) extra old cheddar
½ cup (125 mL) flour
1 tsp. (5 mL) Worcestershire
½ tsp. (2 mL) dry mustard
½ tsp. (2 mL) paprika

Processor method: Cut butter and cheese into chunks. Fit workbowl with steel knife. Place all ingredients into bowl and process for about 30 seconds, or until a soft mass of dough forms. Add extra flour if the dough seems too moist·

Mixer or hand method: Grate cheese very fine. Place all ingredients together in a bowl and beat with a mixer or a wooden spoon until a soft mass of dough forms. Add extra flour if the dough seems too moist.

Both methods continue as follows: Gather the dough into a ball and roll into a sausage shape, about 12 inches long and 1¼ inches in diameter. Chill until very firm.

Cut into slices about ⅛ inch thick. Bake on an ungreased cookie sheet at 350° F for 8-10 minutes, leaving room for the dough to spread as it bakes. Serve warm.

Yield: 4 dozen.
Wine suggestions: Champagne (or your favourite dry bubbly), Vinho Verde

CHEESE STRAWS

½ lb. (250 g) *Quick Puff Pastry*
I egg, beaten

1½ tsp. (7 mL) paprika
¼ lb. (125 g) old Cheddar, grated

Roll out pastry to form a rectangle about 9'' x 15''. Allow the rolled out pastry to rest in the refrigerator for about 1 hour.

Brush pastry with some of the beaten egg.

Blend together the paprika and the cheese. Sprinkle half of this mixture over the pastry. Roll lightly into the surface of the pastry with a rolling pin. Repeat egg wash, sprinkling, and rolling on the other side of the pastry.

Cut pastry into strips about ¼ inch wide. Twist gently into a spiral and place on a foil lined cookie sheet, pressing down ends so that they stay put.

Bake at 450° F for about 10 minutes, or until browned and crisp.

Yield: about 5 dozen.
Wine suggestions: Champagne (or your favourite dry bubbly).

FISH SALAD APPETIZER

1 tbsp. (15 mL) minced onion
1 tbsp. (15 mL) chopped parsley
¼ cup (50 mL) minced celery
2 tbsp. (30 mL) minced carrot
2 hard cooked eggs, grated
¼ cup (50 mL) mayonnaise
1 tbsp. (15 mL) ketchup

½ lb. (250 g) smoked sturgeon (or trout)

Chopped parsley (garnish)

Mix together all ingredients except the sturgeon.

Peel the heavy skin off the sturgeon and chop the flesh quite fine. Stir into the mayonnaise mixture.

The mixture can be shaped into a log and garnished with chopped parsley, then served with crackers.

Yield: About 1½ cups.
Wine suggestions: Amontillado sherry, Gewürztraminer

EGGPLANT APPETIZER

2 lb (1 kg) eggplant
4 cloves garlic

2 tbsp. (30 mL) fresh parsley, minced
1 tomato, chopped
2 scallions, chopped
¼ cup (50 mL) chopped green pepper
¼ cup (50 mL) olive oil
2 tsp. (10 mL) soy sauce
2 tbsp. (30 mL) lemon juice
½ tsp. (2 mL) sugar

Cut eggplant into two, lengthwise. Cut garlic cloves into slices. Make slits in the flesh of the eggplant and insert the garlic slices. Sprinkle the entire surface of the eggplant with salt. Bake at 350°F for 1 hour, or until tender.

When eggplant has cooled slightly, scoop out the flesh with the garlic. Mince very fine, either by hand or with a food processor.

Add the remaining ingredients, and blend together well. Chill thoroughly, then taste and adjust the seasoning if necessary.

Serve with triangles of pita bread.

Yield: about 2 cups.
Wine suggestions: Dry sherry, (e.g. Fino or Amontillado), or a dry Gewürztraminer

SPINACH ROUNDS

1-10 oz pkg. (300 g) frozen spinach, thawed
¼ cup (50 mL) minced onion
⅓ cup (75 mL) fresh parsley, minced
1 tbsp. (15 mL) fresh dill, minced
¼ cup (50 mL) feta, crumbled
½ tsp. (2 mL) dried oregano
¼ lb. (125 g) cream cheese

48 bread rounds (1½ inch diameter)
Grated Parmesan

Squeeze the spinach until completely dry. Chop fine. Combine with onion, parsley, dill, feta, oregano, and cream cheese. Blend well.

Place bread rounds on a cookie sheet. Broil until the top side is browned. Turn over and spread the spinach mixture onto the non-browned side. Sprinkle with grated Parmesan.

Place under the broiler for about 1 minute, or until the spinach is hot and the cheese starts to brown.

Yield: 48 rounds.
Wine suggestions: A medium light white such as Californian Sauvignon Blanc or (brut) sparkling wines or Sylvaner d'Alsace

SHRIMP LOG

½ lb. (250 g) peeled cooked shrimp
2 scallions, minced
1 tbsp. (15 mL) seafood (cocktail) sauce
¼ lb. (125 g) cream cheese

¼ cup (50 mL) fresh parsley, minced

Squeeze moisture out of shrimp. Purée in a food processor, or mince extremely fine by hand.

Combine shrimp purée with scallions, seafood sauce, and cream cheese. Blend together to form a homogenous mixture.

Spoon mixture on to a piece of foil along an imaginary line about 8 inches long. Wrap the foil around the shrimp purée to form a cylinder. Refrigerate until very firm.

Unroll the shrimp "log" onto a serving plate. Pat gently all over with minced parsley. Serve with bread rounds or crackers.

Yield: 1 log (about 1½ cups of purée).
Wine suggestions: Champagne or other dry bubbly; or light, dry white wine such as Chablis, lighter California Chardonnay

OYSTERS FLORENTINE

1½ cup (375 ml) fresh spinach (loosely packed)

½ cup (125 ml) *Mornay Sauce*
Pinch of nutmeg

12 shucked oysters
½ cup (125 mL) fish stock

2 tbsp. (30 mL) Gruyère, grated
1 tbsp. (15 mL) breadcrumbs

Cook spinach in a small amount of water until wilted. Rinse under cold water. Squeeze dry. Chop fine. Combine with Mornay. Season with nutmeg. Set aside.

Drain oysters and cook them in the fish stock over low heat. When the edges of the oysters just begin to curl, remove them with a slotted spoon into a colander to drain. Set aside.

Boil the fish stock remaining in the pan over high heat, uncovered, until it is reduced to a mere 1 tbsp. Pour this 1 tbsp. of concentrated stock into the spinach mixture and stir to blend it in.

Divide the oysters between two ovenproof dishes just large enough to hold them in one layer. Top each dish with half of the spinach mixture. Combine the cheese with the breadcrumbs and sprinkle the mixture over each dish. Bake at 450° F for 5 minutes, or until the sauce is bubbly and the cheese has melted and formed a golden crust.

Yield: 2 servings.
Wine suggestions: light, dry white such as Chablis, Canadian or lighter Californian Chardonnay, or lighter style Gewürztraminer

PISSALADIÈRE

1 pkg. dry yeast	3 tbsp. (50 mL) olive oil
¼ cup (60 mL) lukewarm water	1½ lb. (700 g) onions, sliced
2 cups (500 mL) all purpose flour (approximately)	½ tsp. (2 mL) dried basil
	½ tsp. (2 mL) dried thyme
½ tsp. (2 mL) salt	One 19 fl.oz (540 mL) can tomatoes, drained & chopped
2 tsp. (10 mL) sugar	
1 tbsp. (15 mL) softened butter	1 can flat anchovies, drained
⅔ cup (175 mL) lukewarm water	10 black olives, pitted

Sprinkle the yeast over the ¼ cup of water and let stand for 5-10 minutes. Stir to dissolve.

Stir together the flour, salt and sugar. Combine the yeast, the butter and the remaining water. Add this to the flour mixture, then stir and/or knead until a smooth dough is formed. It should be neither sticky nor dry. Transfer the dough to a buttered bowl, cover with a damp cloth, and leave to rise in a warm place for one hour.

Meanwhile, heat the oil in a 10 inch skillet. Gently cook the onions, along with the basil and thyme, until they are soft and slightly browned.

When the dough has risen, punch the air out of it, roll it out and lay it in a buttered 11-12 inch tart or pizza pan. Spread the onions over the dough. Arrange the tomatoes, the anchovies and the olives attractively over the onions.

Bake at 400° F for 30 to 40 minutes, or until the dough has browned.

Yield: 6-8 servings.
Wine suggestions: Tavel or other rosé; dry or med-dry light-bodied red, such as Lirac

SAVOURY MINI TARTS

Filling of your choice (see below)
1 to 2 dozen mini tart shells

Bake the mini tart shells according to package directions, making sure not to let them get too brown.

Place about 1 tbsp. filling in each baked tart shell.

Bake at 400° F for about 5 minutes, or until filling is bubbly and hot. Serve immediately.

Yield: 1 to 2 doz. tartlets.

Spinach filling: Thaw a 10 oz. pkg. of frozen spinach and squeeze dry. Chop fine. Blend into it the following ingredients: ¼ cup minced onion, ⅓ cup fresh parsley, minced, 1 tbsp. fresh dill, minced, ¼ cup feta, minced, ½ tsp. dried oregano, salt and pepper to taste.

Yield: 1 cup.

Asparagus filling: Drain a 12 fl.oz. can of asparagus and chop fine. Grate ¼ lb. fontina cheese and add to the chopped asparagus, along with ¼ cup drained, chopped pimentos. Make sure the three ingredients are well mixed.

Yield: 1½ cups.
Wine suggestions: a medium-light white such as California Sauvignon Blanc, or (brut) sparkling wines or Sylvaner d'Alsace

MUSHROOM TRIANGLES

4 tbsp. (30 mL) butter
¾ lb. (340 g) mushrooms, chopped
¼ cup (50 mL) scallions, minced
2 tbsp. (30 mL) dry sherry
1 tbsp. (15 mL) flour
¼ cup (50 mL) sour cream
1 tbsp. (15 mL) fresh parsley, minced
Salt and pepper to taste

½ lb (250 g) phyllo dough
¼ lb (125 g) melted butter

Melt the 4 tbsp. butter in a 10 inch skillet. Sauté the mushrooms over very high heat until they have browned. There should be no liquid accumulating in the pan.

When the mushrooms have browned, lower the heat to medium high. Add the scallions and the sherry to the pan, and cook uncovered until the sherry has reduced to almost nothing. Turn down the heat to low.

Stir the flour into the sour cream, along with the parsley. Add to the mushroom mixture, and stir to blend. Taste, and season with salt and pepper. Cook over low heat for a minute or two, then set aside.

Take two sheets of phyllo and lay one on top of the other. Brush the top sheet with melted butter. Cut the dough into six strips, using a sharp knife. Place about one tsp. of filling on the short end of each phyllo strip then fold up each strip to form a triangle. Repeat until all the filling is used.

Brush each triangle with melted butter. Bake at 400° F for 5 to 10 minutes, or until triangles are puffed and golden.

Yield: about 4 doz.
Wine suggestions: Fino sherry, Champagne or other dry bubbly

MUSSELS À LA PROVENÇALE

1 tbsp. (15 mL) butter
2 shallots, minced
1 tomato, diced
2 tsp. (10 mL) tomato paste
2 tbsp. (30 mL) fresh parsley, minced
⅛ tsp. (1 mL) of saffron
⅛ tsp. (1 mL) of thyme
⅛ tsp. (1 mL) of salt
½ cup (125 mL) Rosé wine (e.g. Tavel)

2 dozen mussels

Sauté shallots in butter until soft, but not brown. Add all remaining ingredients except mussels and stir together.

Add mussels, cover pot and cook over medium high heat for about 5 minutes, or until mussels have opened.

To serve, divide both the mussels and the broth between 2 bowls.

Yield: 2 servings
Wine suggestions: Tavel or other rosé; California Sauvignon Blanc

CARAWAY CRACKERS

¼ cup (50 mL) warm water
Pinch of sugar
1 pkg. dry active yeast

2 cups (500 ml) flour
½ tsp. (2 mL) salt
¼ lb. (125 g) butter
½ cup (125 mL) sour cream

1 egg yolk
Caraway seeds

Pour warm water in a small cup with the pinch of sugar. Sprinkle the yeast over the water and let stand for a few minutes until the yeast dissolves and begins to bubble.

Meanwhile, sprinkle the salt over the flour. Cut the butter into the flour until the butter bits are the size of almonds.

Add the dissolved yeast and the sour cream to the butter/flour mixture, and knead until you have a smooth dough. Cover and let stand at room temperature for about 30 minutes.

Roll out ¼ inch thick on a floured board. Brush the dough with the egg yolk, then sprinkle with caraway seeds. Cut into strips (or whatever shape you like).

Bake at 400° F for 8 to 10 minutes.

Yield: 3 to 4 doz.
Wine suggestions: California or German QbA or Kabinett
Riesling, dry bubbly

CARROT VICHYSSOISE

2 cups (500 mL) shredded carrots
2 cups (500 mL) shredded potato
1 cup (250 mL) chopped leeks
1 can chicken broth (10 fl. oz/300 mL) undiluted
2 cups (500 mL) water
1 tbsp. (15 mL) sugar
½ to 1 tsp. (2 to 5 mL) salt

2 cups (500 mL) 35% cream

Place carrots, potato, leeks, chicken broth, water, sugar and salt in a saucepan. Bring to a boil over high heat, then turn the heat to low and simmer, partially covered, for 45 minutes.

Purée contents of saucepan (liquid plus vegetables). Stir in cream.

Best made the day before intended use. Garnish with very fine carrot shreds (a lemon zester scraped against a raw carrot works well).

Yield: 8 servings

Onion Soup au Gratin

1 lb. (500 g) sliced onions
2 tbsp. (30 mL) butter
1⅓ cup (300 mL) canned chicken broth (undiluted)
⅔ cup (200 mL) canned beef broth (undiluted)
2 cups (500 mL) water

1 tbsp. (15 mL) cognac

2 slices bread, toasted
4 oz. (125 g) cheese, grated*

Melt butter in a 10 inch skillet. Cook onions over LOW heat until browned.

Add chicken broth, beef broth and water to skillet and simmer uncovered for about 20 minutes. Add cognac.

Pour soup into ovenproof bowls. Top each with a round of bread large enough to completely cover the bowl. Sprinkle liberally with grated cheese and place under a preheated broiler for 3 to 4 minutes, or until cheese has melted and browned slightly.

Yield: 2 servings

* Suitable cheeses are Swiss, Chedder, Fontina, Jarlsberg, Mozzarella, or any other cheese that melts smoothly and whose flavour you like. Why not try a combination?

MINESTRONE

3 tbsp. (50 mL) butter
½ cup (125 mL) onions chopped
1 cup (250 mL) carrots, diced
1 cup (250 mL) potatoes, diced
½ cup (125 mL) celery, sliced
3 tbsp. (50 mL) flour

One 28 fl.oz.(800 mL) tin
  tomatoes, drained and chopped
8 cups (2 L) chicken stock
¼ cup (50 mL) tomato paste

1 tsp. (5 mL) salt
2 cloves garlic, minced
1 bay leaf
2 tsp. (10 mL) dried oregano
1 tbsp. (15 mL) dried basil

1 cup (250 mL) zucchini, diced
One 14 fl. oz. (400 ml) tin red
  kidney beans, including liquid
  from tin
1 cup (250 mL) pasta
½ cup (125 mL) frozen peas

Melt the butter in a large pot. Add the onions, carrots, potatoes and celery. Toss with a wooden spoon and cook over moderate heat for a minute or so. Sprinkle the flour over the vegetables, and toss so that they are evenly coated.

Add the chopped tomatoes, chicken stock, tomato paste, and seasonings. Bring to a boil over high heat, then reduce heat to low and simmer for about 45 minutes.

With a slotted spoon remove one cup of vegetables from the soup. Purée them, then stir the purée back into the soup.

Add the remaining ingredients and let simmer for about fifteen minutes.

Allow the soup to cool before adjusting any seasonings. The flavours blend and improve with age. Good served with grated parmesan.

Yield: 12 servings

LEEK AND POTATO SOUP

¾ cup (175 mL) sliced onions
1½ cups (375 mL) sliced leeks
4 cups (1 L) shredded potato (about 1½lb or 750 g)
1 can chicken broth (10 fl. oz/300 mL) undiluted
2 cups (500 mL) water
1 tbsp (15 mL) sugar
½ to 1 tsp. (2 to 5 mL) salt

1 cup (250 mL) 35% cream

Combine the onions, leeks, potatoes, chicken stock, sugar, and salt in a saucepan. The liquid will not quite cover the vegetables. Bring the mixture to a boil over medium to high heat, then reduce the heat to low and simmer, partially covered, for 45 minutes. Stir occasionally to prevent burning.

Purée the contents of saucepan (liquids plus vegetables), using a blender or food processor. Blend in the cream.

Serve hot or cold. Best if made the day before intented use. Garnish with freshly cut chives.

Yield: 6 servings

FISH STOCK

2 lb. (1 Kg) fish bones
1 onion, sliced
1 carrot, sliced
½ stalk celery
1 sprig fresh parsley
1 bay leaf
¼ tsp. (2 mL) thyme
2 cups (500 mL) dry white wine
3 cups (750 mL) water
¼ tsp. (1 mL) salt

Place all ingredients in a large pot. Bring to a boil uncovered, then lower heat and simmer uncovered for 1 hour.

Strain. Use immediately, or freeze and use as needed.

Yield: 4 cups

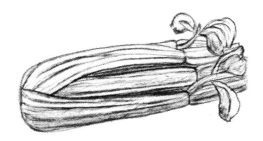

FOUR TREASURE SOUP

4 cups (I L) chicken soup
I tbsp. (15 mL) sherry
2 tsp. (10 mL) soy sauce
2 tsp. (10 mL) sugar
½ tsp. (2 mL) salt

8 dried Chinese mushrooms
¾ cup (175 mL) hot water

One 14 fl. oz. (400 mL) can baby corn cobs
One 5 oz. (142 g) can crab meat
I cup (250 mL) raw spinach, shredded

In a saucepan, combine chicken soup, sherry, soy sauce, sugar and salt. Bring to a boil, then reduce heat to low and allow to simmer.

Meanwhile, soak mushrooms in water until partially softened.

Cut each mushroom into two or three pieces. Put mushrooms and their soaking liquid into the simmering chicken broth.

Add remaining ingredients. Let simmer for about 15 minutes before serving.

Yield: 6 servings
Wine suggestion: A light sherry

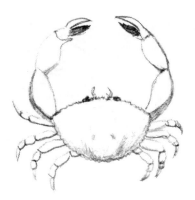

SHRIMP BISQUE

2 tbsp. (30 mL) butter
1 carrot, finely chopped
½ stalk celery, finely chopped
4 scallions, finely chopped
2 tbsp. (30 mL) fresh parsley,
  finely chopped
1 tsp. (5 mL) dried thyme leaves
1 bay leaf
½ tsp. (3 mL) dried tarragon
  leaves
⅛ tsp. (1 mL) saffron

1 tbsp. (15 mL) butter
½ lb. (250 g) shrimp in their
  shell
⅓ cup (75 mL) Cognac

1-19 oz. (540 mL) tin tomatoes,
  drained and chopped
1 cup (250 mL) dry white wine
1 ½ cup (375 mL) fish stock
  (or bottled clam juice)

½ cup (125 mL) 35% cream

In a 3 quart casserole, melt butter over moderate heat. Add carrots, celery and scallions and cook for 2-3 minutes. Remove from heat and stir in parsley, thyme, bay leaf, tarragon and saffron. Set aside.

In a 10 inch skillet, heat butter over moderate heat. Sauté shrimp for about 1 minute. Add Cognac and allow to heat for about 15 seconds, or until warm. Hold a lighted match just over the skillet to flambé.

When flames die down, add shrimp and the pan juices to the large casserole which you have previously set aside. Then add tomatoes, wine and fish stock. bring to a boil, then simmer for 10 minutes over low heat. Remove shrimp. Set aside for another use.

Remove bay leaf from casserole. Purée contents of casserole in a blender or food processor. Strain back into casserole.

Add cream to casserole, stirring to blend with puréed mixture. Heat until hot. Boil over high heat, if desired, for further thickening and/or intensifying of taste.

Portion out into bowls and garnish with the peeled shrimp.

Yield: 3-4 servings

Lentil Soup

½ lb. (250 g) Italian green lentils
8 cups (2 L) water
1-10 fl. oz. (300 mL) can undiluted beef broth

2 tbsp. (30 mL) butter
1 medium onion, chopped
1-19 fl. oz. (540 mL) can tomatoes, drained and chopped
½ tsp. (2 mL) salt
Pepper to taste
½ tsp. (2 mL) dried thyme

Combine water, beef broth and lentils. Bring to a boil. Turn heat to low and simmer for 2-3 hours, or until lentils are tender.

Remove 1 cup of the lentils with a slotted spoon and purée them in a processor blender (or use a food mill or sieve). Return purée to pot and stir to blend.

Melt butter in a skillet or saucepan. Add onions and cook over moderate heat until soft but not brown.

When onions are cooked, add them to the lentils along with the tomatoes and seasonings. Simmer for 15 more minutes.

Yield: 8 servings
Wine suggestions: Sylvaner or Müller-Thurgau

ORANGE SAUCE

1 cup (250 mL) canned beef broth, undiluted
1 cup (250 mL) diluted canned chicken broth
5 tbsp. (75 mL) cornstarch
5 tbsp. (75 mL) cold water

4 tbsp. (50 mL) sugar
4 tbsp. (50 mL) vinegar

½ cup (125 mL) orange juice
1 tbsp. (15 mL) lemon juice
2 tbsp. (30 mL) butter, cut into pieces
4 tbsp. (50 mL) orange flavoured liqueur

Combine beef and chicken broths. Combine cornstarch with water and stir into broth mixture. Heat to boiling, stirring occasionally. Mixture will thicken and become translucent. Set aside: this is your brown sauce.

In another saucepan, heat sugar and vinegar. Bring to a boil over high heat and cook uncovered until mixture has become golden brown. Be careful not to burn it!

Add the brown sauce to the vinegar/sugar mixture. Add juices next, and stir to blend. Whisk in butter pieces.

In a small frypan, boil liqueur until it is reduced to half its original volume. Stir into sauce.

Yield: 2½ cups

Sauce Rouille

1-4 fl. oz. (125 mL) jar pimentos,
½ cup (125 mL) olive oil
2 large garlic cloves
¼ cup (50 mL) dry breadcrumbs

Drain pimentos. Blend together all ingredients in a food processor or blender until a smooth, thick paste is formed.

Serve with bouillabaisse.

Yield: ¾ cup

HOLLANDAISE SAUCE

3 egg yolks
2 tbsp. (30 mL) lemon juice
Dash of cayenne
¼ lb. (125 g) butter, melted

Beat the egg yolks until thick and light yellow. Blend in the lemon juice and cayenne. Slowly add the melted butter, beating constantly. (A food processor or blender does a good job.) When you have added all the butter, the sauce should be thin, but thoroughly emulsified.

Transfer the sauce into the top of a double boiler. Heat over hot (not boiling) water, whisking gently until thick. Sauce should be warm, not steaming hot.

Yield: ¾ cup

BASIC WHITE SAUCE

5 tbsp. (75 mL) butter
5 tbsp. (75 mL) flour
2 cups (500 mL) milk
2 tbsp. (30 mL) minced onion
2 tbsp. (30 mL) minced carrot
2 tbsp. (30 mL) minced celery
¼ tsp. (1 mL) dried thyme

In a saucepan, melt the butter. Add the flour and blend well, making sure there are no big lumps of flour. This is your roux.

Pour in the milk, whisking to blend it thoroughly with the roux. Stir in the chopped vegetables and the thyme. Bring to a boil, stirring occasionally. The sauce will thicken just as it reaches the boiling point. After this point has been reached, lower the heat and simmer for 2 or 3 minutes.

Pass the sauce through a fine strainer, pressing down with the back of a spoon to extract all the flavour from the vegetables.

Yield: about 1½ cups

MORNAY SAUCE

1 cup (250 mL) *Basic White Sauce*
1 cup (250 mL) finely grated Parmesan
½ cup (125 mL) cream

2 egg yolks

Combine white sauce, parmesan, and cream in a saucepan. Cook over medium heat for 3 to 5 minutes, or until cheese has melted and sauce is hot. Stir occasionally to prevent scorching.

Remove saucepan from heat and whisk in egg yolks. Heat very gently making sure the sauce comes nowhere near a boil!

Yield: 2 cups

BASIC BROWN SAUCE

3 tbsp. (50 mL) butter
3 tbsp. (50 mL) flour

One 10 fl. oz. (300 mL) can beef broth
1 tbsp. (15 mL) tomato paste

3 tbsp. (50 mL) minced carrot
2 tbsp. (30 mL) minced onion
3 tbsp. (50 mL) minced celery
¼ tsp. (1 mL) dried thyme

Melt butter in a small saucepan. Add flour, blending to form a roux. Cook over medium heat, stirring occasionally, until the roux browns.

Add the beef broth, *undiluted,* and the tomato paste. Stir with a whisk to completely blend these ingredients with the roux.

Add the minced vegetables and the thyme. Allow the contents of the saucepan to come to a boil, with occasional stirring.

Turn heat to low and simmer for about 10 minutes. Pass the sauce through a fine meshed strainer (such as a chinoise) to remove the vegetables.

Yield: 1 cup

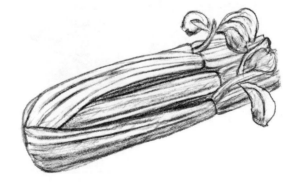

BORDELAISE SAUCE

1 tbsp. (15 mL) butter
1 shallot bulb, minced
¾ cup (175 mL) Bordeaux wine

1 cup (250 mL) *Basic Brown Sauce*

Sauté shallot in butter until limp but not brown. Add wine. Boil uncovered over high heat until reduced by about half.

Add brown sauce and stir to blend. Simmer over very low heat for about 10 minutes.

Yield: about 1⅓ cups

TOMATO SAUCE

1 tbsp. (15 mL) olive oil
1 tbsp. (15 mL) onion, minced
1 tbsp. (15 mL) celery, minced
1 cup (250 mL) canned ground tomatoes
½ tsp. (3 mL) sugar

Place all ingredients together – all at once – in a saucepan. Bring to a boil, then immediately lower the heat and simmer gently for 20 minutes.

Yield: ¾ cup

BOLOGNESE MEAT SAUCE

2 tbsp. (30 mL) olive oil
1 cup (250 mL) chopped onion
½ cup (125 mL) chopped celery
½ cup (125 mL) chopped carrot

¼ lb. (125 g) chopped prosciutto
1 lb. (500 g) lean ground beef

1 cup (250 mL) Barolo wine
1 cup (250 mL) canned crushed tomatoes
½ tsp. (3 mL) oregano
¼ tsp. (1 mL) rosemary
1 tsp. (5 mL) sugar

Heat the oil in a 10 inch skillet. Sauté the vegetables over medium high heat for a few minutes, until the onions begin to soften and turn translucent.

Add the prosciutto and the beef and cook until the beef has browned. Use a wooden spoon to break up the meat as it cooks.

Add the remaining ingredients and simmer gently over low heat for 1 hour. May be used immediately, or else refrigerated or frozen.

Yield: 4 cups

Sauce Mousseline

3 egg yolks
2 tbsp. (30 mL) lemon juice
Dash of cayenne
¼ lb. (125 g) butter, melted

¾ cup (175 mL) whipped cream
(measure after whipping)

In a processor or blender, beat egg yolks with lemon juice and cayenne.

With motor running, pour in melted butter in a slow, steady stream. Continue for about 10 seconds after all butter is added. Stop machine. Sauce should be thin, but thoroughly emulsified.

Transfer sauce into the top of a double boiler. Heat over hot (not boiling) water, whisking gently until thick. Sauce should be warm, not hot.

In a mixing bowl, stir together warm sauce and whipped cream until thoroughly blended. Serve immediately.

Yield: about 1½ cups

PIZZA

1 pkg. dry yeast
¼ cup (50 mL) lukewarm water
3 cups (750 mL) flour (approx.)
½ tsp. (2 mL) salt
1 tbsp. (15 mL) sugar
1 tbsp. (15 mL) oil
1 cup (250 mL) lukewarm water
¼ cup (50 mL) cornmeal

¾ cup (175 mL) *Tomato Sauce*
1 tsp. (5 mL) dried oregano
½ cup (125 mL) mushrooms, sliced
1-14 fl. oz. can (400 mL) asparagus
   tips
2 oz. (60 g) prosciutto
¼ lb. (250 g) fontina cheese
¼ lb. (250 g) mozzarella cheese

Sprinkle yeast over the ¼ cup warm water and let stand for 5-10 minutes. Stir to dissolve.

Stir together flour, sugar and salt. Combine yeast, oil and the 1 cup of water. Add to flour mixture, then stir and/or knead until a smooth dough is formed. It should be neither sticky nor dry.

Divide the dough into two pieces. Roll each into a circle about 12 inches in diameter. Sprinkle two pizza pans with cornmeal, then place dough onto pans.

Spread dough with tomato sauce, then sprinkle with oregano, vegetables and prosciutto.

Shred cheeses, mix together, then sprinkle over each pizza. Bake at 425° F for about 20 minutes, or until cheese has melted and crust has browned.

Yield: 2 large pizzas
Wine suggestion: Chianti, California Pinot Noir, California Zinfandel

FETTUCINE ALFREDO

1½ tbsp. (25 mL) cornstarch
1½ tbsp. (25 mL) cold water

1¼ cup (300 mL) heavy cream
3 oz. (90 g) Parmesan, finely grated
2 oz. (60 g) strong provolone, finely grated
1 tsp. (5 mL) dried oregano
½ tsp. (2 mL) dried basil

½ lb. (250 g) green fettucine

Blend cornstarch and water to form a thin paste. Place in a saucepan, along with the cream, the Parmesan, the provolone, and the herbs.

Bring slowly to a boil over medium heat, stirring occasionally.

Turn heat to low and simmer about 5 minutes. Cheese should be melted and sauce thick enough to coat a spoon.

While sauce is simmering, cook pasta in a large amount of boiling, salted water until just barely tender. Drain well. Combine with sauce and serve immediately.

Yield: 2 servings (main course), 4 servings (side dish)
Wine Suggestions: a fruity white such as Pinot Grigio,
or a light Italian red such as Valpolicella or Chianti

FETTUCINE WITH PEAS AND PIMENTOS

½ lb. (250 g) pasta

1 cup (250 mL) *Basic White Sauce*
½ cup (125 mL) grated Parmesan
2 oz. (60 g) prosciutto, chopped
¾ cup (175 mL) peas
¼ cup (50 mL) pimentos, chopped
½ tsp. (2 mL) dried basil

Boil pasta in a large amount of salted water until cooked "al dente." Drain.

While pasta is cooking, heat white sauce and add to it the remaining ingredients. Simmer together until pasta finishes cooking.

Pour heated sauce over drained pasta. Serve immediately.

Yield: 2 servings
Wine suggestions: a medium weight red such as Vino Nobile di Montepulciano, Chianti Classico, or a lighter California Zinfandel

CHEESE FONDUE

¾ lb. (340 g) Swiss Emmentaler
¼ lb. (125 g) Swiss Gruyère
1 garlic clove
1½ cups (375 mL) dry white wine
2 tbsp. (30 mL) cornstarch
2 tbsp. (30 mL) cold water
Salt, pepper, nutmeg
2-4 tbsp. (30-50 mL) Kirsch

Grate the cheeses and set aside.

Smash the garlic clove gently with the flat of a knife.

Pour the wine into a fondue pot. Combine the cornstarch with the cold water and stir into the wine. Add the garlic clove and the cheese. Heat gently until the cheese melts and the mixture starts to look like a smooth, creamy sauce. If too thin, add equal amounts cornstarch and water (mixed together) and continue heating until thick.

Season with salt, pepper and nutmeg. Add the Kirsch. Let the mixture come to a boil, then remove the garlic clove and place the pot over a lighted burner on the serving table.

Serve with cubes of French bread.

Yield: 2-4 servings
Wine Suggestions: a crisp white such as Swiss Neufchâtel, or Canadian Seyval Blanc

FONDUTA

8 oz. (250 g) fontina cheese
¾ cup (175 mL) milk
4 tbsp. (50 mL) butter

1 tbsp. (15 mL) cornstarch
1 tbsp. (15 mL) water

2 egg yolks

Shred the cheese and place it in a saucepan with the milk and butter.

Combine the cornstarch and water to form a smooth milky liquid, and pour this into the saucepan. Stir to combine it with the other ingredients.

Cook over medium heat, stirring gently while the cheese melts. As the mixture reaches the boiling point, it will become smooth and fairly thick.

As soon as it has reached the boiling point, remove the pan from the heat. Pour some of the cheese mixture into a cup. Add the egg yolks to the cup and stir to blend them with the hot cheese. Then pour the contents of the cup back into the saucepan. Stir to blend.

Serve in small bowls, accompanied by a good white bread.

Yield: 2 servings (main course), 4 servings (appetizer)
Wine suggestions: a light fruity white such as a Pinot Grigio from Grave del Friuli, or a Soave

Eggplant Parmesan

4 cups water (1 L)
1 tbsp. (15 mL) salt

1 lb (500 g) sliced eggplant
¾ cup (175 mL) *Tomato Sauce*
3 oz. (90 g) fontina cheese
3 oz. (90 g) mozzarella cheese

2 tsp. (10 mL) oil

Add the salt to the water and bring to a boil. Place half the eggplant slices in the water and allow to boil for 1 minute. Remove the eggplant from the water and place on a cookie sheet.

Treat the remaining eggplant slices in the same manner, using the same salted water. Pat dry with a clean towel.

Place all the eggplant slices under a preheated broiler and broil for about 5 minutes per side, or until nicely browned on both sides.

Shred the cheeses and toss them together until well mixed.

Use the oil to lightly grease two individual casseroles. (They should hold about one cup when filled). Place a single layer of eggplant slices on the bottom of each casserole. Spread about three tablespoons of tomato sauce over each eggplant layer, followed in each case by about ⅓ cup of the cheese.

Repeat with another eggplant layer, dividing the remaining eggplant between the two casseroles. Now divide the remaining tomato sauce between the two casseroles, and finally the cheese.

Bake at 400° F for 10 to 20 minutes, or until the cheese has melted and the casserole is bubbly and hot.

Yield: 2 servings
Wine suggestions: a medium to full-bodied red such as Chianti Classico, Brunello di Montalcino, Barolo, California Cabernet Sauvignon or a fruity white such as Pinot Grigio

LASAGNA

2 tsp. (10 mL) oil

5 lasagna noodles

4 oz. (120 g) mozzarella cheese
6 oz. (180 g) fontina cheese
2 cups (500 mL) *Bolognese Meat Sauce*

Use the oil to grease the bottom of an 8 inch x 8 inch ovenproof casserole. Set aside.

Boil the lasagne noodles until cooked "al dente." Drain and lay flat on a clean towel. Cut each noodle in half crossways.

Shred both cheeses and toss them together in a bowl so they are well mixed.

Heat the Bolognese meat sauce. Have both the noodles and the cheese nearby.

Assembly: Place 4 noodles, overlapping, on the bottom of the greased casserole. Top with ⅔ of a cup of the meat sauce. Sprinkle with ⅓ of the cheese. Now place 3 noodles, overlapping, so that they completely cover the cheese. Top with another ⅔ cup of sauce, then more cheese (about the same amount as before). Lay the last three noodles, overlapping, to cover the cheese. Cover with the remaining sauce, followed by the remaining cheese.

At this point, the casserole may be refrigerated, or even frozen, if desired. If frozen, thaw before heating.

Bake at 400° F for 20-30 minutes, or until hot and bubbly.

Yield: 4 servings
Wine suggestions: Barolo, Barbaresco or a
California Cabernet Sauvignon, or Zinfandel

RAVIOLI WITH GORGONZOLA

10 oz. (300 g) mini ravioli

1 ½ cup (375 mL) *Basic White Sauce*
4 oz. (120 g) Gorgonzola cheese

2 tsp. (10 mL) dry breadcrumbs

Boil ravioli until cooked "al dente." Drain well.

Heat *Basic White Sauce* with 3 oz. of the Gorgonzola, broken into chunks. Use medium heat and stir often to prevent scorching. Continue heating until the cheese is completely melted.

Add the ravioli to the sauce and stir so that all the ravioli is coated with sauce.

Pour the ravioli and sauce mixture into an ovenproof casserole. Break up the remaining Gorgonzola into small bits, and spread over the top of the casserole. Sprinkle with the breadcrumbs.

Goes beautifully with steamed zucchini.

Yield: 2 servings
Wine suggestions: a light to medium weight red such as Valpolicella, or Chianti, or a California Zinfandel

SALMON WITH DILL SAUCE

2 tbsp. (30 mL) butter
2 tbsp. (30 mL) flour
I cup (250 mL) Fish Stock
I tbsp. (15 mL) fresh dill, minced
I ½ oz. (50 g) dill Havarti, crumbled

I egg yolk
¼ cup (50 mL) heavy cream

2 salmon fillets (6 oz. each, 180 g each.)

Preheat oven to 450° F.

Melt butter in a small saucepan. Add flour, blending to form a roux.

Pour in the fish stock and dill, whisking to blend thoroughly with the roux. Bring to a boil, stirring occasionally. The sauce will thicken just as it reaches the boiling point. At this point, lower the heat and simmer for about 5 minutes.

Add the cheese. Simmer gently and stir occasionally while the cheese melts. Blend the egg yolk with the cream and stir this mixture into the saucepan. Heat gently, preventing the sauce from boiling, as this will curdle the egg yolk. Keep warm while the salmon cooks.

Place fish fillets, skin side down, in a lightly greased baking dish. Bake at 450° F for 10 minutes per inch of thickness of fish.

To serve, pour some sauce onto two heated plates, covering the bottom of each place completely. Add a fish fillet to each. Garnish with a sprig of dill.

Yield: 2 servings
Wine suggestions: a white wine with some herbaceousness, such as Grüner Veltliner, Sauvignon Blanc (French or Californian)

SOLE ALMONDINE

2 sole fillets (4-6 oz. each,) (120-180 g each)

1 tbsp. (15 mL) butter
¼ cup (50 mL) sliced almonds
2 tbsp. (30 mL) dry white wine or lemon juice
½ clove garlic, minced
1 tbsp. (15 mL) fresh parsley, minced

Place fish in one layer in a lightly greased baking dish. Bake at 450° F for about 5 minutes, or until it loses its translucency and becomes chalky white.

Meanwhile, heat the butter in a small frypan, using medium high heat. Sauté the almonds until they start to turn golden brown. Watch carefully: they burn easily! When the almonds are golden, stir in the remaining ingredients, then turn off the heat.

When the fish is done, top each fillet with the almond mixture and serve immediately.

Yield: 2 servings
Wine suggestions: a light crisp white such as Muscadet, Entre-Deux-Mers or Sancerre or a California Sauvignon Blanc

Oven Fried Fillets

2 tsp. (10 mL) oil
½ cup (125 mL) cornflake crumbs
4 tbsp. (50 ml) grated Parmesan
1 tbsp. (15 mL) fresh parsley, minced

1 egg, beaten
2 tbsp. (30 mL) water

2 fish fillets (4-6 oz. each) (120-180 g each)

Combine oil, crumbs, Parmesan and parsley, making sure the oil is blended in well. A food processor is good for this if you have one. Place the mixture on a flat plate.

Combine the egg and water in a shallow dish.

Dip each fillet in the egg mixture, and then in the crumb mixture – just enough to coat both sides.

Bake at 450° F for 10 minutes for every inch of thickness of the fish. (So a fillet that is ½ inch thick will take about 5 minutes to cook). Serve with a slice of lemon.

Yield: 2 servings
Wine suggestions: a medium-light wine such as a white Bordeaux, a Canadian or a lighter style California Chardonnay

SOLE MORNAY

2 sole fillets (4-6 oz. each) (120-180 g each)
½ cup (125 mL) dry white wine
½ cup (125 mL) fish stock

¾ cup (175 mL) *Mornay Sauce*
2 tbsp. (30 mL) grated Gruyère
1 tbsp. (15 mL) breadcrumbs

Place sole fillets in a skillet with the wine. Bring to a boil, uncovered, then reduce heat and simmer for about five minutes, or until the fish loses its translucency and turns a chalky white colour.

Transfer sole to an ovenproof platter just large enough to hold the fish in one layer. Cover with foil to keep warm.

Reduce the wine/fish stock mixture in the skillet to about three tablespoons. Combine with the Mornay Sauce and heat until warmed.

Pour sauce over fish. Sprinkle with cheese and breadcrumbs and place under a heated broiler until bubbly and golden brown.

Yield: 2 servings
Wine suggestions: a crisp white wine such as Chablis, Montagny, Canadian and Californian Chardonnay

SALMON WITH GREEN SAUCE

1½ cups (375 mL) fresh spinach (loosely packed)

2 salmon fillets
½ cup (125 mL) white vermouth
½ cup (125 mL) fish stock
2 tsp. (10 mL) minced shallots
¼ tsp. (1 mL) dried thyme

½ cup (125 mL) 35% cream

Cook spinach in a small amount of water until wilted. Rinse under cold water. Squeeze dry. Set aside.

Place salmon in a 10 inch skillet. Add the vermouth, the fish stock, the thyme and the shallots. Bring to a boil, uncovered, then immediately reduce the heat to low, cover the skillet, and simmer for 5 minutes.

Place fish on a warmed platter and cover with foil to keep warm. Strain the liquid remaining in the skillet, then turn the heat to high and boil briskly, uncovered, until it reduces to ⅓ cup.

Take the reserved spinach and chop it extremely fine, either by hand or with a food processor. Add the cream and reduced cooking liquid and blend well to form a pale green sauce. Return this sauce to the skillet and boil briskly for a minute or two to let it heat and thicken.

Pour a pool of sauce over the bottom of two plates. Place a piece of salmon in the center and serve immediately.

Yield: 2 servings
Wine suggestions: a medium bodied white such as Chablis Grand Cru, Meursault, or California Chardonnay

MOULES MARINIÈRES

4 tbsp. (50 mL) butter
½ cup (125 mL) minced onion
½ tsp. (2 mL) dried thyme
2 tbsp. (30 mL) fresh parsley, minced
½ bottle (375 mL) Chablis or other Chardonnay

3-4 lbs. (1.5-2 Kg) mussels

Sauté onion in butter over medium heat until soft but not brown. Add thyme, parsley, and Chablis.

Add mussels to pot. Raise heat to medium high, cover pot and cook for 5 to 10 minutes, or until mussels open.

Serve each person both mussels and broth, preferably in large soup bowls.

Yield: 2 servings (main course), 4 servings (light lunch or appetizer)
Wine suggestions: Chablis, Meursault, a Chardonnay of your choice

BOUILLABAISSE

¼ cup (50 mL) olive oil
½ cup (125 mL) chopped celery
½ cup (125 mL) chopped carrot
1 cup (250 mL) chopped leeks

2 cloves garlic, minced
½ tsp. dried thyme
Rind of ¼ orange, minced
One 19 oz. (540 mL) can
   tomatoes, drained and
   chopped

3 cups (750 mL) fish stock

1½ cup (375 mL) Tavel or other
   rosé wine
2 tbsp. (30 mL) fresh parsley,
   chopped
½ tsp. (2 mL) saffron threads,
crushed
Salt and pepper to taste

1 live lobster
½ lb. (250 g) lotte or halibut
12 jumbo shrimp
12 large scallops
12 mussels

¾ cup (175 mL) *Sauce Rouille*

Heat the oil. Add the carrots, celery and leeks. Cook over medium heat for about 5 minutes, or until they begin to soften. Add the garlic, thyme, orange rind and tomatoes. Simmer gently for a few minutes.

Transfer the contents of the pot to a food processor or blender. Purée and return to the pot. Add the fish stock, the wine, the parsley, the saffron and salt and pepper if desired. Bring to a boil, then simmer for about 15 minutes.

Add the live lobster and cook for about 3 minutes. Then remove it from the pot and pull the tail section away from the body. Cut the tail lengthwise into half, then add the halves to the pot. Remove the tomalley from the front half of the lobster and stir it into the pot. Pull off the claws, then add them to the pot.

Cut the lotte or halibut into 2 inch chunks. Add it and the remaining fish and seafood to the pot. Simmer ten to 15 minutes longer, or until the fish and seafood is just cooked. Add ¼ cup of the *Sauce Rouille* to pot and stir to blend. Pass remaining sauce separately.

Yield: 4-6 servings
Wine suggestion: a good rosé, such as Tavel

POACHED SALMON

Court Bouillon:
8 cups (2 L) water
4 cups (1 L) dry white wine
2 onions, quartered
2 stalks celery, coarsely chopped
1 large carrot, coarsely chopped
4 sprigs parsley

½ tsp. (3 mL) dried thyme
6 peppercorns
1 tsp. (5 mL) salt

Fish:
3-5 lb. (1.5-2.5 Kg) whole salmon

Combine ingredients for court couillon in a large poacher. Bring to a boil, then simmer for 20 minutes.

Meanwhile: Wrap fish loosely in cheesecloth, allowing enough cheesecloth on each end to hang over the poacher. (These will be used later as "handles" to pick up the fish.) Lay the fish on its side. Measure it at its thickest point.

Remove the vegetables and herbs from the court bouillon. Immerse the fish in the bouillon. The liquid should completely cover the fish; if it doesn't, add water. Bring to a boil again over medium heat.

As soon as it reaches the boiling point, reduce the heat to low, cover, and cook the fish in the simmering (not boiling) bouillon for 10 minutes per inch of thickness of the fish.

Remove the fish from the poacher, using the cheesecloth "handles" to help.

Lay the fish on a serving platter. Open the cheesecloth and pull it out from under the fish. Remove the skin with a small knife. It should come off easily. Wipe the platter clean with paper towels. Garnish the fish and platter as desired. A simple way is to place a row of thinly sliced cucumbers along the length of the fish. On each slice of cucumber, place a halved cherry tomato, cut side down.

Yield: 3-5 servings
Wine suggestions: a medium weight white Alsatian Riesling, Meursault, or a Graves

POACHED SALMON
WITH TARRAGON SAUCE

1 cup (250 mL) water
2 cups (500 mL) dry white wine
½ onion, sliced
1 stalk celery, sliced
2 sprigs parsley
1 tsp. (5 mL) dried tarragon
¼ tsp. (1 mL) salt

2 tbsp. (30 mL) butter
2 tbsp. (30 mL) flour
¾ cup *Fish Stock* or clam juice
¼ cup (50 mL) 35% cream

¼ cup (125 mL) dry white wine
2 tsp. (10 mL) dried tarragon

2 salmon steaks or fillets

In a saucepan, combine the first seven ingredients. Bring to a boil, then simmer uncovered for 20 minutes. Strain into a 10 inch skillet. This is your "court-bouillon."

Place the fish in a single layer in the court-bouillon. The bouillon should completely cover the fish. If it doesn't, add water. Bring to a boil again over medium heat. As soon as it reaches the boiling point, reduce the heat to low, cover, and cook the fish in the simmering bouillon for 10 minutes per inch of thickness of fish.

Meanwhile, prepare the sauce: In a saucepan, melt the butter. Stir in the flour and cook, stirring for about 30 seconds. Add the clam juice and stir with a whisk to form a smooth mixture. Bring to a boil, and simmer for a minute or two. Stir in the cream. Set aside.

In another saucepan, bring the wine and the tarragon to a boil over high heat. Continue to boil uncovered until the wine is reduced to about two tablespoons. Pour into the reserved sauce, and stir to blend. Keep warm until needed.

When the fish is done, remove it from the skillet with a broad spatula. Place on warmed plates, wiping with a paper towel if any poaching liquid collects on the plate. Pour some sauce over each piece of salmon and serve immediately.

Yield: 2 servings
Wine suggestions: a white such as Grüner Veltliner, Seyval Blanc or Sauvignon Blanc

SEAFOOD STRUDEL

3 cups (750 mL) cooked seafood

5 tbsp. (75 mL) butter
5 tbsp. (75 mL) flour
1½ cup (375 mL) 10% cream
½ cup (125 mL) grated Parmesan

1 tbsp. (15 mL) butter
½ cup (125 mL) scallions, minced
½ cup (125 mL) Chablis or other
   Chardonnay
½ tsp. (2 mL) dry mustard
Pinch of pepper
⅛ tsp. (1 mL) saffron threads,
   crushed
¼ tsp. (1 mL) thyme

¼ cup (50 mL) dry breadcrumbs
¼ cup (50 mL) grated Parmesan
12 sheets phyllo dough
¼ lb. (125 g) melted butter

If seafood seems excessively wet, drain or squeeze out the excess water. Chop into small pieces, if necessary. Set aside.

In a saucepan, melt the butter. Stir in the flour and cook, stirring, for about 30 seconds. Add the cream and stir with a whisk or spoon to form a smooth mixture. Bring to a boil and simmer for a minute or two. Stir in the Parmesan, cover, and set aside.

In a 10 inch skillet, melt the 2 tbsp. of butter over medium heat. Add the scallions and cook, stirring occasionally, until they are soft but not brown. Add the wine to the skillet and raise the heat to high. Boil briskly, uncovered, until the wine is reduced to about two tablespoons. Stir in the spices. Add the seafood and just enough of the sauce to bind it together.

Combine the breadcrumbs and the Parmesan. Set aside. Stack two sheets of phyllo on a clean towel. Brush with melted butter. Repeat this operation two more times, so that you end up with 6 layers of phyllo. Use the other 6 sheets the same way, stacking them on another towel. Sprinkle the top layer of both phyllo stacks with some of the reserved breadcrumb mixture.

Spoon half of the filling along the shorter edge of one of the phyllo stacks. Use the remaining filling in the same way on the other phyllo stack. Using the towel to help you, roll up each phyllo stack around the seafood mixture. Brush the top of each roll with melted butter and sprinkle with some of the breadcrumbs.

Transfer to a greased cookie sheet and bake at 375° F for 30 minutes, or until crisp and golden.

Yield 6 servings
Wine suggestions: Grand Cru Chablis, Meursault or other relatively full bodied Chardonnay

LOBSTER IN WHITE WINE SAUCE

6 live lobsters, 1 ¾ lb. females
Water
½ tsp. (2 mL) salt

5 tbsp. (75 mL) butter
5 tbsp. (75 mL) flour
1 ½ cups (375 mL) 10% cream
½ cup (125 mL) grated Parmesan

2 tbsp. (30 mL) butter
½ cup (125 mL) scallions, minced
½ (125 mL) Chablis
½ tsp. (2 mL) dry mustard
Pinch of pepper
⅛ tsp. (1 mL) crushed saffron threads
¼ tsp. (1 mL) thyme

2 slices white bread
¼ cup (50 mL) parsley
2 tbsp. (30 mL) oil

Lie three of the lobsters on their back. Place a wooden spoon on the underside of each and secure it with kitchen string in 3 or 4 places.

Add about 3 inches of water to a large pot. Add salt. Bring to a boil over high heat, then add the lobsters. When water returns to a boil, reduce heat, then cover and steam lobsters for 20 minutes. Repeat this entire operation for the remaining lobsters.

When lobsters are cool enough to handle, remove spoons and string. Twist off the claws and crack them. Remove meat from claws. dice and set aside. Using kitchen scissors cut a 2 inch wide opening down the back (top) surface of each lobster. Remove all the meat, dice and set aside. Discard the eye sac, the coral and greenish tomalley.

In a saucepan, melt the butter. Stir in the flour and cook, stirring, for about 30 seconds. Add the cream and stir with a whisk to form a smooth mixture. Bring to a boil and simmer for a minute or two. Stir in the Parmesan, cover, and set aside.

In an 8-10 inch skillet, melt the 2 tbsp. butter over medium heat. Add the scallions and cook, stirring occasionally, until soft but not brown. Add wine to skillet. Reduce over high heat until almost dry. Stir in spices. Add lobster meat and then the reserved sauce. Stir until well mixed. Stuff mixture back into lobster shells.

With a food processor (or by hand) chop bread and parsley until finely chopped. Add oil and process or work with fingers until crumbs are coated evenly. Sprinkle over stuffed lobsters. You may stop at this point and refrigerate the lobsters.

Place stuff lobsters on baking sheets and bake at 400° F for 20 minutes, or until stuffing bubbles and topping is browned. Transfer to a serving platter and serve immediately.

Yield: 6 servings
Wine suggestions: big Chardonnays such as Grand Crus Chablis, California Chardonnay; or Gewürztraminer

ANDALUSIAN SCALLOPS

1 scallion, minced
4 oz. (125 mL) jar roasted sweet peppers (red)
1 tbsp. (15 mL) tomato paste
1 tbsp. (15 mL) ground almonds
2 tbsp. (30 mL) sherry
⅛ tsp. (1 mL) saffron threads, crushed

12 oz. (340 g) scallops
4 tbsp. (50 mL) sherry

Blend together first 6 ingredients using a food processor or blender. Set aside.

In an 8-10 inch skillet, over medium heat, simmer the scallops with the sherry. In one or two minutes the scallops should become opaque and firm (but not hard and rubbery!) Remove the scallops at this point; and set aside.

Turn the heat up to high and let the liquid in the skillet evaporate until almost nothing is left. Lower the heat and add the sauce. When hot, put the scallops back into the skillet (using a slotted spoon), stir to combine with the sauce and serve immediately.

Yield: 2 servings
Wine suggestion: Sherry
(fino or amontillado)

CHICKEN CACCIATORE

3 lb. (1.5 Kg) chicken, cut up
¼ cup (50 mL) flour
2 tbsp. (30 mL) oil

¼ lb. (125 g) mushrooms, cut in quarters
¾ cup (175 mL) onions, sliced
1 green pepper, chopped
½ cup (125 mL) sliced celery
½ cup (125 mL) chopped pepperoni
1 clove garlic, minced

1½ cup (375 mL) ground peeled tomatoes
½ tsp. (3 mL) oregano
½ tsp. (3 mL) rosemary
Salt and pepper to taste
¼ cup (50 mL) red vermouth

Coat chicken with flour. Tap off excess. Brown in hot oil, then transfer to an ovenproof casserole.

Pour most of the oil out of the pan. Sauté mushrooms over high heat until browned. Lower heat to medium-high. Add onions, green pepper, celery, pepperoni and garlic to pan. Sauté 2 to 3 minutes, or until vegetables are slightly softened.

Add remaining ingredients to pan and bring to a boil. Pour over chicken.

Cover casserole and bake at 350° F for about 1¼ hours.

Yield: 4 portions
Wine suggestions: a full bodied red such as Barolo, Barbaresco; or California Zinfandel or Cabernet Sauvignon

PINK PIQUANT CHICKEN

2 chicken breasts (skinned and deboned)
1 egg, beaten
1 tbsp. (15 mL) milk
½ cup (125 mL) breadcrumbs

2 tbsp. (30 mL) butter

¾ cup (175 mL) 35% cream
1 scallion, minced
1 tsp. (5 mL) tomato paste
2 oz. (60 g) cheese: ½ oz. (15 g) Roquefort, crumbled,
    ½ oz. (15 g) old cheddar, crumbled, 1 oz. (30 g)
    Parmesan, grated

Fresh parsley for garnish

Combine beaten egg with milk. Dip chicken in egg mixture, then in breadcrumbs.

Heat butter in a skillet. Sauté chicken on both sides just until browned. Place in an ovenproof dish and bake at 400° F for 10-15 minutes, or until the juices run clear when the chicken is pierced with a knife.

Meanwhile, pour the cream into a clean skillet. Add the scallion, the tomato paste and the cheeses. Bring to a boil over high heat, then lower the heat and simmer until the cheeses have melted.

When the chicken is done, pour some sauce over the bottom of a plate to form a thin "pool," then place a chicken breast on it. Garnish with a sprig of fresh parsley.

Yield: 2 servings
Wine suggestions: a medium weight red wine such as Moulis, Vino Nobile di Montelpulciano, or Beaujolais Crus, or California Merlot

SZECHWAN CHICKEN

½ lb. (250 g) deboned chicken breasts
1 tbsp. (15 mL) cornstarch
1 tbsp. (15 mL) oil

¼ tsp. (1 mL) salt
4 scallions, chopped
2 tbsp. (30 mL) fresh ginger root, minced
1 tsp. (5 mL) fresh garlic, minced

2 tsp. (10 mL) Chinese chili paste
1 tbsp. (15 mL) ketchup
1 tsp. (5 mL) soy sauce
1 tbsp. (15 mL) dry sherry
½ tsp. (2 mL) sugar

Cut chicken into slivers. Combine chicken and cornstarch, so that chicken slivers are well coated with the cornstarch. Heat the oil in a wok, then add the chicken and stir-fry for two to three minutes, or until the chicken is done. Remove the chicken from the wok.

Add the salt, scallions, ginger root and garlic to the wok. Stir-fry for about 30 seconds, adding extra oil if needed.

Return the chicken to the wok. Stir to blend with the scallion mixture.

Combine the remaining ingredients in a small bowl, then pour the mixture into the wok. Toss together with the chicken and scallions so that everything is well coated.

Serve with boiled rice: this dish is spicy!

Yield: 2 servings
Wine suggestions: a sweet white wine with good acidity such as
Gewürztraminer, Bonnezeaux, Coteaux de Layon, or Late Harvest Riesling.

CHICKEN PAPRIKASH

3 lb. (1.5 Kg) chicken, cut up
¼ cup (50 mL) flour
2 tbsp. (30 mL) oil

2 cups (500 mL) onions, sliced
2 tbsp. (30 mL) paprika

½ cup (125 mL) chicken stock

2 tbsp. (30 mL) cornstarch
2 tbsp. (30 mL) cold water
1 cup (250 mL) sour cream

Coat chicken with flour, tapping off excess. Brown floured chicken in oil over high heat. Remove browned pieces from pan and set aside.

Pour most of the oil out of the pan, leaving only a thin film. Turn the heat down to medium and sauté the onions until lightly browned.

Remove pan from heat. Stir in the paprika so that the onions are well coated. Add the chicken stock, then return the pan to the heat and bring its contents to a boil.

Return the chicken to the pan. Turn the heat down to low and simmer the chicken, covered, for 45-60 minutes, or until the juices run clear when the chicken is pierced with the tip of a sharp knife.

When done, remove the chicken pieces to a serving platter. Skim the surface fat from the pan.

Dissolve the cornstarch in the water and stir this mixture into the pan. Turn the heat up to medium high and bring to a boil, so that juices thicken. Stir in the sour cream and heat only until the sauce is hot through and through. Do not boil. Taste for seasoning and add extra paprika, if desired. Pour over chicken and serve.

Yield: 4 servings
Wine suggestions: a medium dry white wine with definite flavour, such as a Gewürz-traminer

GRATIN AU BLEU

2 tbsp. (30 mL) butter
2 tbsp. (30 mL) flour
¾ cup (175 mL) chicken stock
3 oz. (90 g) Cambozola cheese
¼ cup (50 mL) 35% cream

1½ cup (375 mL) cooked diced chicken

1 slice white bread
2 tbsp. (30 mL) fresh parsley
1 tbsp. (15 mL) oil

In a saucepan, melt butter. Stir in the flour and cook, stirring, for about 30 seconds. Add the chicken stock and stir with a whisk to form a smooth mixture. Bring to a boil and simmer for a minute or two.

Add the cheese, cut up in pieces, and the cream. Simmer over low heat until the cheese is melted, stirring occasionally.

Add the chicken and stir to blend with the sauce. Pour into an ovenproof casserole.

In a food processor (or by hand) combine the bread and the parsley and process until fine crumbs are formed. Add the oil and process just until blended with the crumbs. Sprinkle this topping over the chicken and sauce.

Bake in a 450° F oven for 15 to 20 minutes or until hot and bubbly.

Yield: 2 servings
Wine suggestions: A medium light red such as Beaujolais (Crus) or Mâcon or Chianti; or a lightweight Cabernet Sauvignon

Chicken Parmesan

2 chicken breasts, skinned and boned
1 egg, beaten
½ cup (125 mL) cornflake crumbs

¾ cup (175 mL) *Tomato Sauce*
2 oz. (60 g) mozzarella, shredded

Coat each piece of chicken with egg, then pat with crumbs. Put into a lightly greased baking dish, just large enough to hold them in a single layer.

Bake at 400° F for 10 to 15 minutes, or until juices are clear when the chicken is pierced with a sharp knife.

Remove chicken from oven and turn on broiler. Add sauce to chicken, then top with cheese. Place under broiler just until sauce is bubbly and cheese has melted.

Yield: 2 servings
Wine suggestions: a light Italian red, such as Valpolicella or Bardolino; or a Beaujolais-Villages

DUCK WITH PORT SAUCE

1 duckling

½ cup (125 mL) Port
1 cup (250 mL) *Basic Brown Sauce*

Preheat oven to 450° F.

Pat duckling completely dry with paper towels. Truss it with kitchen cord. Prick holes in the skin around the breast and thighs, using a fork or the point of a knife.

Place the duckling, breast side up, on a rack set in a shallow roasting pan. Pour about ½ inch of water into the bottom of the pan. Roast in the middle of the oven for 30 minutes.

While the duck is roasting, make the sauce: In a small saucepan, boil the port over high heat until it is reduced to about ¼ cup. Add to it the brown sauce, and stir to blend. Set aside until serving time.

When the first 30 minutes of roasting are up, lower the heat to 350° F, turn the duckling on its side and roast for an additional 30 minutes. Then turn the bird on its other side and continue roasting for another 30 minutes. Finally turn it breast side up again for 30 minutes.

To test for doneness, pierce the thigh of the duckling with the point of a knife: the juice that runs out should be yellowish, with no trace of pink.

Using poultry shears, cut the duckling into quarters, and serve with the port sauce.

Yield: 4 servings
Wine suggestions: a full-bodied red such as a fine Bordeaux or a Californian Cabernet Sauvignon, or a Maréchal Foch

CHICKEN BREASTS WITH TARRAGON SAUCE

2 single chicken breasts, skinned and deboned
2 tbsp. (30 mL) butter, melted

2 tbsp. (30 mL) butter
2 tbsp. (30 mL) flour
¾ cup (175 mL) chicken stock
¼ cup (50 mL) heavy cream

¼ cup (50 mL) dry white wine
2 tsp. (10 mL) dried tarragon leaves

Place chicken breasts in a baking dish. Pour over melted butter, covering the chicken completely. Bake in a preheated 450° F oven for 10 to 15 minutes, or until the juices are clear when the meat is pierced with a knife.

Meanwhile prepare the sauce: In a saucepan, melt the 2 tbsp. butter. Stir in flour and cook, stirring, for about 30 seconds. Add the chicken stock and stir with a whisk to blend with the butter-flour mixture. Bring to a boil, then turn down the heat to low and simmer for 2 or 3 minutes. Stir in cream and set aside.

In another saucepan, bring the wine and the tarragon to a boil. Continue to boil until the wine is reduced to about 2 tbsps. Pour in the reserved sauce and stir to blend. Keep warm until the chicken is ready.

To serve, place a chicken breast on each plate, and pour some sauce over each, so that the sauce coats the chicken completely.

Yield: 2 servings
Wine suggestions: White wines with a herbaceousness nature such as Sauvignon Blanc, or white Bordeaux

COQ AU RIESLING

1 chicken, about 3 lb. (1.5 Kg)
Flour
2 tbsp. (15 mL) oil
1 tbsp. (15 mL) butter
1 shallot, minced
1 clove garlic, minced
1½ cups (375 mL) Alsatian Riesling

1 tbsp. (15 mL) butter
1 tbsp. (15 mL) flour
1 cup (250 mL) 35% cream
1 tbsp. (15 mL) minced parsley
1 tbsp. (15 mL) minced scallion
  green
Salt and pepper to taste

Cut chicken into quarters. Sprinkle with flour, then tap off excess. Heat oil in a 10 inch skillet and brown chicken until golden. Remove chicken and pour off any excess fat.

Melt butter, and lightly sauté the shallot and garlic, being careful not to let them burn. Return the chicken to the skillet, and pour in the wine. Bring to a boil, then turn heat down to low, cover the pan, and allow the contents to simmer for 50 to 60 minutes, or until chicken is tender and juices run clear when pierced with a knife. Remove chicken from skillet and keep warm.

Turn heat up to high and boil the liquid in the skillet, uncovered, until reduced to one cup.

In a small dish, mash together the butter and flour until they are well blended. Add this to the liquid in the skillet and blend with a whisk. Add the cream, the parsley and the scallion green, and allow to simmer for two or three minutes. Season to taste with salt and pepper.

Put the chicken back into the skillet, coating each piece thoroughly with the sauce. Serve immediately.

Yield: 4 servings
Wine suggestion: Alsatian Riesling

CHICKEN IN PASTRY

2 single chicken breasts, deboned
2 tbsp. (30 mL) butter, melted

4 oz. (120 g) pâté de foie
½ lb. (250 g) *Quick Puff Pastry*

1 egg, beaten

Place chicken breasts in an ovenproof dish. Pour melted butter over chicken breasts and bake in a preheated 450° F oven for 8 minutes. Cool slightly.

Using a cheese slicer, scrape thin slices off the pâté. Cover the top of the chicken breasts with these slices. You should only use half the pâté for this operation. Reserve the other half for later.

Divide the pastry into 4 equal pieces. Roll out each into a rectangle about ¹⁄₁₆ of an inch thick. Cut each piece of pastry in half, so that you have two somewhat square pieces from each.

Place each chicken breast, pâté side down, on a piece of pastry. Cut the pastry around the chicken, leaving a ½ inch border all around.

Cover the top of the chicken breasts with the remaining pâté, in a manner similar to before.

Cover the chicken breasts with the remaining pastry pieces. Trim, leaving a margin ¾ inch wider than the bottom piece of pastry. Tuck this top piece of pastry under the bottom one. Decorate top as desired with pastry scraps.

Brush entire surface of pastry with beaten egg. Bake on a foil-lined cookie sheet at 450° F for 20-25 minutes.

Yield: 2 servings
Wine suggestions: a full-bodied wine with a lot of acidity such as a Tokay d'Alsace or a big California Chardonnay

GRENOUILLES AU RIESLING

12 frog legs
1 tsp (15 mL) butter
1 shallot, minced
1 clove garlic, minced
⅔ cup (150 mL) Alsatian Riesling
⅓ cup (100 mL) chicken stock

2 tsp (10 mL) soft butter
2 tsp (10 mL) flour
½ cup (125 mL) 35% cream
2 tsp (10 mL) minced parsley
1 tbsp (15 mL) minced scallion
(green portion)
Salt and pepper to taste

Cut each pair of frog legs in half at the joint between the legs. Set aside.

In a skillet, melt the butter over medium-high heat and sauté the shallot and garlic for a minute or so being careful not to let them brown. Add the frog legs, the wine and the chicken stock to the skillet. Bring to a boil, then immediately turn the heat down to low, cover the skillet, and allow the contents to simmer for about 10 minutes or until the meat is cooked.

Remove the frog legs onto a platter with a slotted spoon and cover with foil to keep warm while you prepare the sauce. Turn heat up to high and boil the liquid in the skillet uncovered until reduced by about one-third.

In a small dish, mash together the butter and flour until they are well blended. Add this to the liquid in the skillet and blend with a whisk. Add the cream, the parsley and the scallion tops, and allow to cook for two or three minutes. Season to taste with salt and pepper.

Put the frog legs back into the skillet. Stir gently to coat them thoroughly with the sauce and serve immediately.

Yield: 2 servings (main course), 4 servings (appetizer)
Wine suggestion: Alsatian Riesling

DUCKLING À L'ORANGE

2 oranges
2 ducklings

2 ½ cups (625 mL) *Orange Sauce*

Preheat oven to 450° F.

Pat ducklings completely dry with paper towels. Cut the oranges in half and place 2 halves inside each duckling. Truss the ducklings with kitchen cord.

Prick holes in the skin around the breast and thighs of each duckling, using a fork or the point of a knife.

Place the ducklings, breast side up, on a rack set in a shallow roasting pan. Pour about ½ inch of water into the bottom of the pan. Roast in the middle of the oven for 30 minutes.

At this point, lower the heat to 350° F, turn the ducklings on their sides and roast for an additional 30 minutes. Then turn the birds on their other side and continue roasting for another 30 minutes. Finally turn them breast side up again for 30 minutes. To test for doneness, pierce the thigh of each duckling with the point of a knife: the juice that runs out should be yellowish, with no trace of pink.

Using poultry shears, cut the ducklings in quarters, discarding the oranges that were inside.

Place the pieces of duckling attractively on a serving platter. Pour a light coating of orange sauce over top. Scatter finely julienned orange peel (use a zester) over the pieces of duckling. Put paper frills on the legs. Line the border of the platter with orange slices and place a half maraschino cherry on each slice. Extra sauce may be served separately.

Yield: 8 servings
Wine suggestions: A full-bodied red such as Hermitage, or Côte Rôtie or a fine Bordeaux; or a big, oaky California Chardonnay

Spanish Lamb Stew

2 tbsp. (30 mL) oil
1 lb. (500 g) lamb cubed
Flour
1 onion, sliced
1 large potato, diced
1 large green pepper, cut in strips
2 oz. (60 g) serrano ham, cubed *

4 fl. oz. jar (125 mL) pimentos, drained
4 tsp. (20 mL) tomato paste
1 tbsp. (15 mL) ground almonds
¼ cup (50 mL) red Rioja

Heat oil. Coat lamb with flour and brown in hot oil. Remove and place in oven-proof casserole.

Using more oil if necessary, fry onion and potato over medium heat for 2-3 minutes. Add to casserole along with pepper and ham.

Purée pimento and combine with remaining ingredients. Add to casserole. Bake at 325° F for 30 to 40 minutes, or until meat is tender and done to taste.

*   or substitute prosciutto.

Yield: 4 servings
Wine suggestions: medium-full reds such as Rioja
or Cabernet Sauvignon

LEG OF LAMB IN WINE SAUCE

1 leg of lamb
1 cup (250 mL) Bordeaux
½ cup (125 mL) beef broth
½ tsp. (2 mL) Worcestershire

⅛ tsp. (1 mL) of sugar
2 tbsp. (30 mL) cornstarch
2 tbsp. (30 mL) cold water
1 tbsp. (15 mL) butter

Have your butcher take the bone out of the leg of lamb and cut the bone into pieces; then reshape the meat and tie it so that it holds its shape. The meat should be covered with a layer of removable fat.

Place the bones in a shallow roasting pan with an onion that has been quartered but not peeled. Roast at 450° F until bones have browned. Remove browned bones and onion from roasting pan and place them into a stock pot. Cover with water, add ¼ tsp. salt, and simmer for a few hours, or until you reach a flavour concentration that you like. Strain through a chinoise or very fine mesh and set aside.

In a saucepan, reduce the Bordeaux to ½ cup. To this reduced wine, add 2 cups of the lamb stock, the ½ cup beef broth, the Worcestershire and the sugar. Mix together the cornstarch and water, and stir into the saucepan while the contents are still cool. Bring to a boil, stirring occasionally, then cook for a minute over low heat. Whisk in the butter. Set aside until the roast is served.

To roast the lamb, place in a shallow roasting pan in a 425° F oven. Allow to roast undisturbed for about 1¼ hours. At this time, test for doneness and continue cooking according to how well done you like your meat.

When done, let the meat sit at room temperature for about 10 minutes before serving. Remove the layer of fat from the meat then slice and serve with the sauce.

Yield: 8 servings
Wine suggestions: Cabernet Sauvignon, especially Bordeaux

VEAL MARSALA

good 10/18/92

¾ lb. (340 g) veal scallopini
Flour
2 tbsp. (30 mL) butter

½ cup (125 mL) dry Marsala
½ cup (125 mL) chicken stock
2 tsp. (10 mL) butter

Pound veal until paper thin. Dredge with flour, shaking off excess.

Sauté veal in butter about 30 seconds on each side. Transfer to a warmed platter and cover with foil to keep warm.

Add Marsala and chicken stock to pan and boil briskly for a few minutes, scraping any fragments clinging to the bottom of the pan. Continue boiling (uncovered) until liquids have reduced to about one half cup. Whisk in butter.

Return veal to pan, turning to coat with sauce and reheat if necessary. Serve immediately.

Yield: 2 servings
Wine suggestions: medium weight dry reds such as Vino Nobile di Montepulciano, or Beaujolais Crus

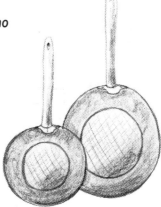

BOEUF BOURGIGNON

1 lb. (500 g) lamb, cubed
1 bottle Burgundy wine
4 tbsp. (50 mL) butter

4 oz. (120 g) bacon
3 tbsp. (50 mL) flour
2 tbsp. (30 mL) tomato paste
24 tiny white onions
1 large carrot, sliced
½ lb. (250 g) mushrooms,

2 cloves garlic, minced
Pinch of pepper and salt
¼ tsp. (1 mL) sugar
½ tsp. (2 mL) dried thyme
1 bay leaf
¼ cup (50 mL) brandy

Marinate meat in ½ of the wine for 12 hours. Strain, reserving the marinade. Pat meat dry with paper towels.

In a skillet, melt butter. Add meat to skillet, in batches if necessary, and brown meat on all sides. As they are browned, place them in a large saucepan or casserole.

In a separate 10 inch skillet, cook the bacon until crispy. Remove the cooked bacon with a slotted spoon and add to the casserole with the browned meat.

To the fat remaining in the skillet (there should be about 3 tbsp.), add the flour. Blend well to form a roux, and cook until the roux is a nice brown colour. Add the marinade and the tomato paste, and stir to blend with the roux. Boil for 2-3 minutes, uncovered. Add to casserole.

Add the remaining wine to the casserole, along with the onions, the carrot, the mushrooms, and the seasonings. Bring the contents of the casserole to a boil, then reduce the heat to low and simmer partially covered for 2 hours, or until the meat is tender.

Skim off the fat, if necessary. Add the brandy and boil the contents of the pot, uncovered, until the sauce reaches the desired thickness and taste intensity.

Yield: 6 servings
Wine suggestions: traditionally Burgundy, but also California Cabernet or Canadian Maréchal Foch

STEAK AU POIVRE

1 tbsp. (15 mL) green peppercorns
2 filet mignons (6 oz. each, 180 g each)
2 tbsp. (30 mL) butter

2 tsp. (10 mL) vinegar
2 tsp. (10 mL) sugar
1 cup (250 mL) *Basic Brown Sauce*
6 tbsp. (100 mL) heavy cream
Pinch of ground pepper
1 tbsp. (15 mL) Cognac

Crush peppercorns with a rolling pin or the flat of a knife. Press evenly into both sides of the steaks.

Heat butter in a small skillet. Cook steaks in butter over medium high heat. After about 5 minutes, turn the steaks, lower the heat to low and cook another 5 minutes or until done to taste.

Meanwhile, prepare the sauce: In a saucepan, heat the vinegar and sugar until the sugar dissolves and turns a golden brown colour. Add the remaining ingredients and simmer together for a few minutes.

To serve, pour the sauce over the bottom of two heated plates, so that the plate is covered. Place a steak on the center of each plate.

Yield: 2 servings
Wine suggestion: Cabernet Sauvignon

VEAL WITH TARRAGON SAUCE

¾ lb. (340 g) veal scallopini
Flour
2 tbsp. (30 mL) butter

⅔ cup (150 mL) Madeira
⅓ cup (75 mL) chicken stock
One finely minced shallot
½ tsp. (2 mL) dried tarragon leaves

2 tsp. (10 mL) butter

Pound veal until paper thin. Dredge with flour, shaking off excess.

Sauté veal in butter, about 30 seconds on each side. Transfer to a warmed platter and cover with foil to keep warm.

Add next 4 ingredients to skillet and boil briskly, uncovered, over high heat until volume has reduced to ½ cup.

Strain into a clean skillet and whisk in butter. Return meat briefly to pan, turning to coat with sauce. Serve immediately.

Yield: 2 servings
Wine suggestions: either a full bodied white with definite flavour such as Tokay d'Alsace; or a light red, such as Valpolicella

Veal à la Crème

2 tbsp. (30 mL) butter
12 oz (340 g) veal filet

2 tbsp. (30 mL) butter
4 oz. (120 g) mushrooms, sliced

½ oz. (15 g) Pipo Crème, crumbled
1 oz. (30 g) old Cheddar, grated
⅔ cup (150 mL) cream
2 scallions, finely minced
Pinch of freshly grated nutmeg

Slice veal into medallions, about one inch thick. Sauté veal in butter over medium-high heat for 2 minutes each side, until about half cooked. Cover and set aside over lowest possible heat.

Using an 8-10'' skillet, sauté the mushrooms in butter over high heat until nicely browned. Add the remaining ingredients, and heat together, stirring, until the cheese has melted and the sauce is hot. Continue cooking, uncovered, until the taste intensity and the thickness are to your liking.

Yield: 2 servings
Wine suggestions: a medium weight red such as Vino Nobile di Montepulciano or Chianti Classico or a California Merlot

STEAK CHASSEUR

2 tbsp. (30 mL) butter
2 filet mignons (6 oz. each, 180 g each)

3 tbsp. (50 mL) butter
1 tbsp. (15 mL) minced shallots
6 oz. (180 g) mushrooms, sliced

⅔ cup (150 mL) white (suggest Muscat d'Alsace)
1 cup (250 mL) *Basic Brown Sauce*
Pinch of tarragon
1 tbsp. (15 mL) tomato paste
1 tsp. (5 mL) cassis

Heat the butter in a skillet. Brown the meat on one side over medium heat, and continue to cook for about 5 minutes. Turn over, reduce the heat to low, and continue to cook while preparing the sauce.

Heat the remaining butter in a skillet over high heat. Sauté the shallots and mushrooms until golden. Remove them from the skillet. Add the wine and reduce it to ¼ cup.

Add back the mushrooms and shallots, along with the remaining ingredients, stirring to blend. Cook until heated through. Pour some sauce over the bottom of each plate, then place a steak in the center of each plate. Good accompanied by wild rice and green beans.

Yield: 2 servings
Wine suggestions: a full bodied red such as Côtes du Rhône or Australian Shiraz or Californian Merlot or a fine Bordeaux or Burgundy

STEAK IN PASTRY

2 tbsp. (30 mL) butter (approx.)
4 filet mignons (4-5 oz. each, 120-150 g each)
12 sheets phyllo dough
Melted butter
4 tbsp. (50 mL) breadcrumbs
1 recipe *Sauce Bordelaise*

Heat butter in a 10'' skillet. Sauté steaks over high heat until seared on both sides, but NOT cooked through and through.

Lay two sheets of phyllo on top of each other. Brush the top sheet only with melted butter. Sprinkle 1 tbsp. of the breadcrumbs over an area about the size of a steak in the center of one edge of phyllo. Place a sautéed steak on top of the breadcrumbs. Roll the phyllo and the steak to form a cylinder with the steak enclosed in the center and two ends of phyllo extending on both sides. cut the ends so they extend only about three inches. Tuck each end under the steak.

Take a new sheet of phyllo and brush it with melted butter. Now place the ''steak package'' in the center of this buttered phyllo sheet and draw the phyllo up all around the ''package.'' Arrange the excess dough attractively over the top of the ''steak package.'' Brush the whole exterior with melted butter. Repeat the phyllo stacking and steak wrapping procedure for the other three steaks. Place the four packages on a lightly greased cookie sheet. They may be refrigerated at this point if desired.

Heat the oven to 375° F and bake for 15 minutes for medium rare beef. While the meat is cooking, heat the Sauce Bordelaise. To serve, pour a thin layer of sauce over the surface of each plate, then place the steak package in the center of the plate.

Yield: 4 servings
Wine Suggestion: Cabernet Sauvignon, especially one from Bordeaux

FRICASSÉE OF RABBIT

1 rabbit, cut into parts
Flour
2 tbsp. (30 mL) butter

1 small onion
½ cup (125 mL) chicken stock
1 cup (250 mL) Madeira
½ tsp. (2 mL) dried tarragon

1 cup (250 mL) mushrooms, quartered
⅓ cup (75 mL) heavy cream

Coat meat lightly with flour. Sauté in butter, using a 10" skillet. Add onion, chicken stock, Madeira, and tarragon. Bring to a boil then reduce heat to low and simmer covered for 1½ hours, or until meat is tender.

Remove meat and keep warm. Strain into a measuring cup. You should have about 1¾ cups of liquid. Pour the liquid back into the skillet and add the mushrooms. Raise the heat to high and reduce the liquid to about one cup (not counting the mushrooms).

Mash together the 1 tbsp. butter with the 1 tbsp. of flour. Remove the skillet from the heat and blend in the butter-flour mixture. Then put the skillet back on the heat and stir until thickened. Stir in the cream.

Add the meat back to the skillet, and simmer for an additional 5 minutes.

Yield: 4 servings
Wine suggestions: a softer style medium weight red such as Vino Nobile di Montepulciano, or a Cabernet Sauvignon or Merlot

VEAL AUX POMMES

2 tbsp. (30 mL) butter
1 tbsp. (15 mL) brown sugar
2 medium apples
Nutmeg to taste

¼ cup (50 mL) Calvados
¾ cup (175 mL) 35% cream

2 tbsp. (30 mL) flour
12 oz. (340 g) veal scallopini
2 tbsp. (30 mL) butter

Heat butter in a 10" skillet over medium heat. Add sugar and stir until it is melted.

Peel, core and slice the apples. Add the apple slices to the skillet and stir gently to coat them with the butter/sugar mixture. Cover the skillet and let the apples cook for about 5 minutes, or until they are almost (but not completely) soft.

Season with nutmeg. Add the Calvados. Turn the heat to high and boil uncovered until the Calvados is thick and syrupy. Add the cream and cook uncovered until the sauce has thickened slightly.

Coat the veal with the flour, shaking off any excess. In a new skillet, heat the butter and sauté the veal quickly on both sides until done. This should only take a few minutes.

Add the cooked veal to the sauce and allow to simmer together for one or two minutes.

Yield: 2 servings
Wine suggestions: Apple cider; or a medium weight, medium dry white wine such as Australian Semillon, Côtes de Bordeaux or Graves Supérieure

VEAL CACCIATORE

2 tbsp. (30 mL) oil
6 oz. (180 g) mushrooms

½ cup 125 mL) sliced onion
3 small zucchini (or 1 regular), cut into chunks

1 oz. (30 g) prosciutto, chopped
¼ cup (50 mL) dry Marsala
⅓ cup (75 mL) beef broth
¾ cup (175 mL) *Tomato Sauce*
1 fresh tomato, cut into wedges

8 oz. (250 g) veal scallopini
Flour
2 tbsp. (30 mL) oil

Sauté the mushrooms in the oil over high heat until they have turned a golden brown colour.

Lower the heat to medium. Add the onions and the zucchini to the skillet, and cook for 2 to 3 minutes, or until they begin to soften.

Add the remaining ingredients, stirring gently to combine them. Simmer over low heat for 10 minutes. If the sauce gets too thick, you may add water.

When the sauce is just about ready, coat the veal lightly with flour, shaking off the excess. Using a separate skillet, sauté the veal in oil, cooking it for only a minute or so on each side. When the veal is done, add it to the sauce, and let it simmer in the sauce for a minute or so. Serve with Italian Rissotto (rice) or buttered pasta.

Yield: 2 servings
Wine suggestions: Valpolicella, or Merlot from Italy,
France or California

VEAL WITH TUNA SAUCE

1 tsp. (5 mL) capers
1 tin tuna (6½ oz/185 g)
3 anchovy fillets
2 egg yolks
3 tbsp. (50 mL) lemon juice

¾ cup (175 mL) oil

3 lb. (1.5 Kg) boneless veal roast
1 bottle Italian white wine (Pinot
   Grigio from Friuli area)
1 onion, sliced
1 celery stalk, sliced
1 carrot, sliced
Water, as needed

Place the first five ingredients into a food processor or blender and purée.

With the motor running, gradually add the oil. Keep blending until you have a homogeneous sauce, the consistency of a thick mayonnaise. Place in a jar or container and set aside.

Place the veal in a pot just large enough to hold it comfortably. Add the remaining ingredients, using only enough water to ensure that the meat is covered. Bring to a boil, then lower the heat and simmer for 2 hours.

Remove from the heat and allow the veal to cool in its own broth. Remove it from the broth, trim the fat, if any, and any strings holding it together. Slice and serve with the tuna sauce.

Goes well with marinated vegetables and fresh tomatoes.

Yield: 6 servings
Wine suggestions: a light red such as Grignolino or Bardolino; or a light fruity white such as Pinot Grigio, Soave or California Sauvignon Blanc

Beef with Red Peppercorns

1 tbsp. (15 mL) butter
2 filet mignons (180 g each)

2 tbsp. (30 mL) butter
2 tbsp. (30 mL) scallions, (including green part)

2 tsp. (10 mL) red peppercorns
2 tbsp. (30 mL) Cognac

½ cup (125 mL) 35% cream
Salt and pepper to taste

In a small skillet heat the 1 tbsp. of butter. Brown the steaks on one side over medium heat, and continue to cook for about 5 minutes. Turn over, reduce the heat to low, and continue to cook while you prepare the sauce.

In a 10'' skillet, melt the rest of the butter over medium high heat. Sauté the scallions, then add the red peppercorns and the Cognac. Turn the heat up to high and boil the Cognac for a minute or so to evaporate the alcohol.

Now add the cream, and season to taste with salt and ground pepper. Boil gently for one or two minutes, stirring so that the ingredients are well mixed.

To serve, place a steak on each plate and pour some sauce over the top.

Yield: 2 servings
Wine suggestions: a medium to full bodied red such as most Cabernet Sauvignons, Morgon or Moulin à Vent

POTATOES - RIOJA STYLE

1½ lb. (750 g) potatoes

1 tbsp. (15 mL) oil
1 chorizo sausage
1 onion, chopped
1 clove garlic, minced
½ tsp. (2 mL) salt or to taste
¼ tsp. (1 mL) sugar
½ tsp. (2 mL) paprika

1 sweet red pepper

Peel potatoes. Cut into chunks and place in a bowl of water.

In a large pot, heat oil over medium-high heat. Slice chorizo and add it to the pot, along with the onion. Let cook until lightly browned. Add garlic, salt, sugar and paprika, stirring to blend with onion and sausage.

Place potatoes in pot and add enough water to cover them by about an inch or two. Bring to a gentle boil, then cook uncovered until the potatoes are tender. When the potatoes are almost done, add the red pepper cut into strips.

When serving, make sure each person receives potato, vegetables and broth.

Yield: 4 servings
Wine suggestions: red Rioja or California Cabernet Sauvignon or Canadian Maréchal Foch

MOLDED POTATOES

2 tbsp. (30 mL) softened butter
2½ lb. (1 Kg) baking potatoes
1 cup (250 mL) thinly sliced leeks
1½ cup (375 mL) shredded Cheddar
Salt, nutmeg
6 tbsp. (100 mL) melted butter

Generously grease a 1½ quart pyrex mixing bowl with softened butter. Slice the potatoes paper thin. Line the bowl with potato slices, overlapping them slightly to form a pattern of concentric circles. Pour some of the melted butter over the potatoes.

Fill the bowl with alternating layers of potato, leeks, cheese, butter and seasonings, making sure to start and end with a potato layer. By the time you finish, the bowl should be slightly overfilled and the contents packed down well.

Bake at 450° F for 1¼ hours, or until a knife inserted into the centre meets no resistance. Remove from oven.

Let the bowl and its contents rest for 5 minutes. Then check with the point of a knife to make sure the potatoes are not stuck to the bowl. Unmold onto a serving plate, wipe up excess butter and serve immediately.

Note: The same recipe can be made using individual molds, such as custard cups. Reduce the baking time according to the size of the mold, using the same test for doneness described above.

Yield: 8 servings

SPINACH SALAD

2 cups (500 mL) fresh spinach
¾ cup (175 mL) drained lychee nuts
½ cup (125 mL) cherry tomatoes

1 tsp. (5 mL) soy sauce
1 tbsp. (15 mL) vinegar
1 tsp. (5 mL) sugar
2 tsp. (10 mL) sesame oil
1 tbsp. (15 mL) juice from lychees

Wash and dry spinach. Tear into bite size pieces. Cut lychee nuts in half. Cut cherry tomatoes in half if they are on the large size. Toss together the tomatoes, lychees and spinach in a salad bowl.

In a cup or small dish, mix together the soy sauce, vinegar, sugar, sesame oil and lychee juice.

Pour this dressing over the ingredients in the salad bowl and serve immediately.

Yield: 2-4 servings

PARSLEY CARROTS

⅓ cup (75 mL) water (approx)
1 tbsp. (15 mL) butter
Pinch of salt
½ tsp. (3 mL) sugar

1 cup (250 mL) sliced or julienned carrots

1 tbsp. (15 mL) fresh parsley

Place water, butter, salt and sugar in a saucepan. Heat until butter melts and salt and sugar dissolve.

Add carrots. Bring to a boil over moderate heat and simmer partially covered for 5 to 8 minutes. Cooking time will vary according to the thickness of the carrot slices and also according to taste. By the time the carrots are tender-crisp, the water should be almost evaporated. If the mixture becomes too dry before the carrots are tender, you may add a small amount of extra water.

Just before the carrots are ready to serve, stir in the chopped parsley.

Yield: 2 servings

CAESAR SALAD

1 clove garlic, crushed
2 tbsp. (30 mL) vinegar
¼ tsp. (1 mL) salt
¼ tsp. (1 mL) dry mustard
Dash of Worcestershire sauce
1 tin anchovies, drained and chopped fine

⅓ cup (75 mL) olive oil

1 head romaine lettuce
1 egg yolk, beaten lightly
½ cup (125 mL) grated Parmesan
1 cup (250 mL) croutons

Place the garlic, vinegar, salt, mustard, Worcestershire and anchovies together in a salad bowl. Stir so that they become well blended.

Add the oil slowly, beating it well into the vinegar mixture.

Tear the lettuce into bite size pieces. Add the lettuce to the salad bowl and toss with the dressing.

Add the egg to the salad bowl and toss again. Then add the Parmesan and the croutons and toss until well mixed.

Yield: 4 servings

SPINACH WITH PINE NUTS

2 pkgs. fresh spinach (10 oz/300 g)
1 tbsp. (15 mL) butter
¼ cup (50 mL) cup pine nuts or sliced almonds
Salt and pepper

Wash spinach. Drain or spin dry.

In a wok or skillet, melt butter over high heat. Sauté pine nuts until golden brown. Remove from wok and reserve.

Add spinach to wok (or skillet), tossing so as to cook quickly and evenly. Cook until just barely wilted. It should take only a few minutes. If your pan is not large enough to accommodate all the spinach at once, you can do this operation in two batches.

Toss pine nuts back into spinach. Season to taste with salt and pepper, and serve immediately.

Yield: 6 servings

MELLOW YELLOW RICE

1 ½ cups (375 mL) long grain rice
⅛ tsp. (1 mL) tumeric
2 ¾ cups (400 mL) cold water

Place rice in saucepan. Add tumeric and water. Bring to a boil, uncovered, over high heat. Continue to boil, uncovered, until you begin to see crater-like holes on the surface of the rice.

Turn the heat down to the lowest it goes. Cover the saucepan and let stand undisturbed for about 15 to 20 minutes, or until the rice is tender and all the water is absorbed. Fluff up with a fork.

Yield: 6 servings

PEAS WITH PROSCIUTTO AND PEPPERS

2 tbsp. (30 mL) butter
¼ cup (50 mL) chopped onion

2 oz. (60 g) prosciutto
4 oz. (125 mL) roasted sweet (red) peppers
2 cups (500 mL) frozen green peas
2 tbsp. (30 mL) water

Sauté onion in butter over medium heat until soft but not brown.

Chop prosciutto into small pieces. Drain peppers and chop finely.

Add prosciutto and peppers to sautéed onions, along with peas and water. Cook uncovered for three to four minutes or until peas are cooked and water has evaporated.

Yield: 4 servings

Sweet Potatoes and Carrot Purée

1 lb. (500 g) sweet potatoes

½ lb. (250 g) carrots
¾ cup (175 mL) water

2 tbsp. (30 mL) butter
Salt to taste
Nutmeg to taste

Scrub and dry potatoes. Pierce with a fork. Bake at 400° F for 45 minutes to 1 hour or until tender when pierced with the tip of a pointed knife. Time will vary according to the size of the potatoes.

Meanwhile, peel and slice carrots. Place them in a 10 inch skillet with the water. Bring to a boil, uncovered, over high heat. Then reduce heat to low and simmer, partially covered, for about 30 minutes or until carrots are tender and all the liquid has evaporated.

When the potatoes are done, scrape out the flesh and place along with the cooked carrots into a food mill or processor. Purée. Blend in butter and season to taste with salt and nutmeg.

Serve immediately or place in an ovenproof serving dish and refrigerate. Later reheat at 400° F for about 20 minutes or until hot.

Yield: 4 servings

DILL-icious Artichoke Salad

2 tbsp. (30 mL) lemon juice
1 tbsp. (15 mL) oil
1 tbsp. (15 mL) fresh dill, finely chopped

One 14 fl. oz. (400 mL) can whole artichoke hearts

Combine lemon juice, oil and dill in a mixing bowl.

Drain artichokes. Cut each one in half vertically.

Add artichokes to dressing. Toss briefly. Chill for at least 30 minutes before serving, to allow flavours to blend.

Yield: 2 servings

SCALLOPED POTATOES

2 tbsp. (30 mL) butter
2 cups (500 mL) sliced leeks

5 (8. oz /250 g) baking potatoes
1½ cup (375 mL) shredded Jarlsberg
1½ cup (375 mL) milk or 10% cream
Salt
Nutmeg

Use ½ tbsp. of the butter to grease a baking dish approximately 7" x 11" in size.

Melt the remaining butter in a skillet and sauté the leeks over medium heat until soft but not brown.

Peel the potatoes and slice paper thin (1/16 inch). Place a layer of overlapping slices over the bottom of the baking dish, using approximately one third of the potato slices. Sprinkle with one third of the leeks and ½ cup of the cheese. Sprinkle lightly with salt and nutmeg. Repeat these layers twice more, so that your finished dish has 3 layers of potato, each topped with leeks, cheese and seasoning. Heat the milk or cream and pour it into the baking dish.

Bake at 450° F for 30-40 minutes or until the potatoes are tender when pierced with a knife.

Yield: 8 servings

Green Beans Almondine

1 tbsp. (15 mL) butter
¼ cup (50 mL) sliced almonds
2 tbsp. (30 mL) white wine, lemon juice or sherry
½ clove garlic, minced
1 tbsp. (15 mL) fresh parsley, chopped

One 10 oz. (300 g) package frozen green beans,
   thawed and drained, or 2 cups fresh green beans,
   steamed or boiled uncovered until tender-crisp

Heat butter in a saucepan over medium-high heat. Fry almonds until they start to turn golden brown. Watch them carefully: they burn easily. When the almonds are golden, stir in the wine, garlic and parsley.

Immediately add the thawed green beans. Cook and stir until the green beans are heated through, about 2-5 minutes.

Yield: 4 servings

PEAR SHERBET

1 ½ cups (375 mL) water
1 cup (250 mL) sugar
3 ripe pears
1 tsp. (5 mL) vanilla
1 lemon

Bring the sugar and water to a boil stirring occasionally until the sugar dissolves. Boil briskly, uncovered, for exactly 4 ½ minutes, timing from the point at which the mixture begins to boil. Set aside.

Peel and quarter pears. Place in a saucepan with just enough water to cover them. Bring to a boil uncovered, then simmer for about 6 minutes, or until the tip of a knife inserted into a pear meets no resistance.

Drain the pears and purée. You should have about 1 cup of purée. Blend in the vanilla, along with the juice of the lemon, and the sugar solution.

Pour into a shallow pan and freeze until almost firm. Then remove from freezer, and either whip with electric beaters or process with the steel knife of a food processor. Spoon at once into serving dishes, or into paperlined muffin tins (to be used at a later date).

Use this dish to refresh the palate between courses,
or as a summer dessert.
Either way, it is best enjoyed alone.

Yield: 6 servings

PEARS IN RED WINE

2 Barlett pears (6 oz each) (180 g each)

⅓ cup (75 mL) sugar or to taste
1 cup (250 mL) Bordeaux wine

Make sure that pears are nice and ripe. Peel them and cut each in half lengthwise. Use a small spoon to scoop out the core from each half.

Bring sugar and wine to a boil. Simmer pears uncovered until tender, about 20 minutes. Time will vary according to the ripeness of the pears. Turn pears over occasionally while cooking.

When pears are tender, remove saucepan from the heat. Cover and allow pears to remain in wine at room temperature for about 3 hours. At this point they may be served, or refrigerated until needed. Serve with cheese, if desired.

Yield: 4 servings
Wine suggestions: a very fruity red such as Australian Shiraz or Californian Cabernet Sauvignon or Merlot

KIWI SHERBET

1½ cups (375 mL) water
1 cup (250 mL) sugar
3 large kiwi
1 tsp. (5 mL) vanilla
1 lemon

Bring the sugar and water to a boil stirring occasionally until the sugar dissolves. Boil briskly, uncovered, for exactly 4 ½ minutes, timing from the point at which the mixture begins to boil. Set aside.

Peel and trim the kiwi. Purée the peeled fruit. You should have about ¾ cup. Blend in the juice of the lemon, the vanilla and the sugar solution.

Pour into a shallow pan and freeze until almost firm. Then remove from freezer, and either whip with electric beaters or process with the steel knife of a food processor. Spoon at once into serving dishes, or into paperlined muffin tins (to be used at a later date).

Use this dish to refresh the palate between courses, or as a summer dessert. Either way, it is best enjoyed alone.

Yield: 6 servings

SWEET PASTRY DOUGH

1½ cup (375 mL) all purpose flour
¼ lb. (125 g) unsalted butter

3 egg yolks
1 tsp. (5 mL) vanilla extract
6 tbsp. (100 mL) sugar
⅛ tsp. (1 mL) salt

Cut together the flour and butter until the butter is broken into small bits the size of peas and each bit is coated with flour. This may be done with two knives as for pastry or with a food processor. Transfer to a large mixing bowl and set aside.

In a small bowl, blend together the egg yolks, the vanilla, the salt and the sugar. Pour into the butter-flour mixture and blend with your fingertips until it begins to form a ball.

Transfer the mass to a floured board. Using a sliding motion with the heel of your hand, push the pastry, a small portion at a time, away from you along the board. Then gather up all the pieces to form a ball. It should be smooth, well mixed, and quite soft. Wrap and refrigerate until firm.

Use as directed in pastry recipes.

Yield: 1 lb. dough or 5 individual shells (4" diameter)

FRESH FRUIT TART

1 recipe *Sweet Pastry Dough*
1 tbsp. (15 mL) butter

1½ cup (375 mL) fresh fruit *
6 tbsp. (100 mL) sugar
1 tbsp. (15 mL) Kirsch
1 to 1½ tbsp. (15-20 mL) cornstarch
1 to 1½ tbsp. (15-20 mL) cold water

Butter a 9 or 10 inch flan ring (quiche type pan). Roll the dough until it is slightly larger than the size of your pan, and line the pan with the dough.

Using a knife, trim the pastry so that it is flush with the top of the pan. Cover the dough with foil and weigh down the foil with dried beans. Bake at 400° F for about 10 minutes, or until the pastry is set. Remove the beans and the foil, and continue baking another 5 to 10 minutes, or until nicely browned.

When done, let cool for 10 to 15 minutes, then remove the pastry from the pan and set it on a rack to cool completely.

While the pastry is baking, prepare the filling: Slice the fruit if necessary. Place it in a saucepan with the sugar and the Kirsch and heat over medium high heat until juices start to collect in the bottom of the pan. At this point, combine the cornstarch with the cold water and stir it vigorously into the saucepan. Continue heating until the fruit has softened slightly and the juices have thickened. Remove from the heat and cool.

Assemble the tart by spreading the filling over the bottom of the pastry.

* Avoid banana, pineapple and citrus fruits.

Yield: one 9-10" tart or 5 individual 4" tarts
Wine suggestions: a dessert wine such as Barsac, Late Harvest Riesling from Canada or California, German beerenauslese, trockenbeerenauslese or Eiswein

APPLE BLUEBERRY SAUCE

⅓ cup (75 mL) liqueur of your choice
¼ cup (50 mL) sugar
1 tbsp. (15 mL) butter
¼ tsp. (1 mL) cinnamon

5 apples, peeled and cored
½ cup (125 mL) blueberries
1 tbsp. (15 mL) cornstarch
1 tbsp. (15 mL) cold water

Heat liqueur, sugar, butter and cinnamon in a 10 inch skillet and stir until sugar dissolves and butter melts.

Slice apples and add to skillet along with blueberries (if fresh blueberries are not available, frozen ones will do). Cover pan and simmer until apples are tender.

Dissolve cornstarch in water. Stir into cooked fruit mixture, using only as much as is needed to thicken the juices in the pan.

Cook the mixture one more minute to make sure the starch is thoroughly cooked.

May be refrigerated and reheated if desired. Good poured over ice cream, or by itself with whipped cream; or poured into baked pastry shells.

Yield: 6 servings

Wine suggestions: a sweet wine such as a German Auslese or a sweet California Riesling; or a dessert sherry; or for something different try a Moulin Touchais

CHOCOLATE TRUFFLES

6 oz. (180 g) bittersweet chocolate
2 egg yolks
4 tbsp. (50 mL) unsalted butter (softened)

Rind of ½ orange
2 tbsp. (30 mL) Grand Marnier

Cocoa

Melt chocolate and allow it to cool to room temperature. In a food processor or blender (or by hand), blend the chocolate with the egg yolks until well combined. Add the butter, in pieces, and blend again until the mixture is perfectly smooth.

Finally, blend in the orange rind, which should be finely grated or chopped, and the Grand Marnier. Pour the mixture into a bowl, cover with plastic wrap, and refrigerate until it is firm enough to be handled and shaped.

Form into balls by rolling about a teaspoonful in the palms of your hands. Roll each ball in cocoa.

Yield: 1½ -2 dozen
Wine suggestions: wine generally not recommended, but if you must serve something try a Ruby Port or Vintage Character Port, or a Late Harvest Zinfandel

QUICK PUFF PASTRY

2 cups (500 mL) all purpose flour
¼ tsp. (1 mL) salt
½ lb. (250 g) unsalted butter

½ -¾ cup (125-175 mL) cold water

Cut butter, flour and salt together (by hand or with a processor) until the butter bits are the size of almonds. Place in a large mixing bowl.

Gradually add water, stirring with a fork or your fingers as you pour, so that the water is evenly incorporated into the flour and butter mixture. Use as much water as is necessary to form a moist, but not sticky, dough.

Form into a ball with your hands. Wrap and refrigerate for about 30 minutes before rolling.

Roll dough into a rectangle with a long edge in front of you. Fold one short side into the center of the rectangle. Now fold the other side in, so that both sides now meet in the center. Fold dough in half, using the line where your two sides meet as the hinge. This rolling and folding procedure is called "one turn."

With a narrow side facing you, roll the dough into a rectangle, shaped so that the narrow edge is always facing you. Fold as before (narrow edges into the center).

Do at least one more turn, preferably two. It is advisable to wrap the dough and refrigerate it for 30 minutes in between turns.

Yield: 1½ lb. dough

TARTE AU FROMAGE

½ recipe *Quick Puff Pastry*
4 oz. Gorgonzola cheese
5 oz. Boursin (garlic/fine herbs)
½ cup heavy cream

1 tbsp. fresh parsley

Roll out pastry to ⅛ inch thickness. Let rest in refrigerator for about 1 hour. Trim with a knife so that you form an 8'' x 12'' rectangle. Place on a foil lined cookie sheet. Prick holes all over the pastry with a fork. Bake at 350° F for about 30 minutes, or until browned through and through.

Whip cream until stiff. Add cheeses, broken first into half-inch pieces. Whip again until you have a smooth mixture. Refrigerate until ready to use.

When pastry is completely cool, spread the cheese mixture over it, then sprinkle with parsley. If desired, place halved grapes all the way around the edges, on top of the cheese mixture.

Serve at room temperature. Cut with a serrated knife.

Yield: 4 servings
Wine suggestions: sweet dessert wines such as Sauternes, Canadian or California Late Harvest Riesling or German beerenauslese or trockenbeerenauslese.

EASY APRICOT TARTS

1 recipe *Quick Puff Pastry*
1 egg, beaten
2 oz. (60 g) marzipan
Two-14 fl. oz. (400 mL) cans apricots
¼ cup (50 mL) apricot glaze

Roll out pastry to form a rectangle about 12" x 18". Cut 3" rounds from the rolled out pastry. Place each circle of pastry on a cookie sheet and brush each one lightly with beaten egg, being careful not to spill egg over the edges of each circle.

With the marzipan, make little balls about the size of large green peas. Place one of these marzipan balls in the center of each circle of pastry and press down lightly.

Drain the apricots. Place one apricot half, round side up, over each marzipan ball. There should be a rim of pastry still showing all around the apricot.

Bake at 400° F for about 25 minutes, or until the pastry has browned and has puffed up around the apricot.

Heat the apricot glaze and brush the apricot on each tart with the warmed glaze.

Yield: about 18 tarts
Wine suggestions: a dessert wine, such as Sauternes, Riesling Auslese or Beerenauslese, Muscat Beaumes de Venise or Canadian or Californian Late Harvest Riesling

CRÊPES SUZETTE

3 eggs
2 tbsp. (30 mL) oil
½ cup (125 mL) Grand Marnier

¾ cup (175 mL) all purpose flour
2 tbsp. (30 mL) sugar
1 cup (250 mL) milk

Rind of half orange, chopped
6 tbsp. (100 mL) sugar
¼ lb. (125 g) butter
1 cup (250 mL) orange juice
2 tbsp. (30 mL) lemon juice
¼ cup (50 mL) Grand Marnier
Extra oil for greasing pan

Beat the eggs lightly. Stir in the oil and the ½ cup of Grand Marnier.

Add the flour and the sugar and mix well to form a thick, smooth paste. Finally, pour in the milk, and stir just long enough to form a thin, lump-free batter. DO NOT OVERMIX. Let stand for an hour or so before using.

Heat a crêpe pan, greased as necessary, over medium high heat until a drop of water flicked onto it splutters and evaporates instantly. Stir the crêpe batter lightly. Pour enough batter into the pan to almost fill it. Immediately pour the batter back into the bowl, leaving only a thin film covering the bottom of the crêpe pan. Cook the crêpe for a minute or so, until the rim begins to turn brown. Loosen the edges, then turn out onto a clean towel. Do not cook the second side. Repeat this procedure until all the batter is used up. Crêpes may be refrigerated for a few days, or frozen for long term storage.

To prepare the sauce: Place the sugar and the rind in a skillet and heat until sugar starts to melt and turn golden yellow. Add the butter and allow it to melt. Don't worry if the sugar crystallizes – it will eventually melt again. Add the juices and boil the mixture briskly, uncovered, until it reduces to a syrupy consistency. May be made ahead and refrigerated, then reheated.

Final assembly: Fold each crêpe into quarters and place them in the sauce, turning them so they are thoroughly coated. Heat the Grand Marnier in a small saucepan, ignite it and quickly pour it over the crêpes. Bring the dish to the table flaming.

Yield: 6 servings
Wine suggestions: a lush dessert wine such as Sauternes or California Late Harvest Riesling; or else, try Grand Marnier

Bibliography

Amerine, Maynard A. & Edward B. Roessler. *Wines Their Sensory Evaluation*. San Francisco, W. H. Freeman and Company, 1976.

Boni, A. *Italian Regional Cooking*. New York, Bonanza Books, 1969.

Brillat-Savarin, *The Physiology of Taste*. New York, Dover, 1960.

Broadbent, M. *Wine Tasting*. London, Christie's, 1979.

Cooper, D. *Wine with Food*. New York, Crescent Books, 1980.

Currle, O. *The Classic Vines are Coming Back*. German Wine Review, 1984/I.

Duijker, H. *The Great Wines of Burgundy*. New York, Crescent Books, 1982. English translation Mitchell Beazley, 1983.

Finger, H. *Rhenish Hesse - a wine paradise*. German Wine Review, 1980/II.

Fischer, A. *Le Gastronomie Alsacienne - Saisons d'Alsace,* Strasbourg, 1969.

Fowler, N. *German Wine Atlas*. London, Mitchell Beazley, 1980.

Freson, R. et al. *The Taste of France*. Stewart, Tabori and Chang.

Fuchss, P. *The Rhenish Palatinate Wine-growing Region*. German Wine Review, 1981/I.

Hanson, A. *Burgundy*. London, Faber & Faber, 1982.

Hazelton, N. *The Cooking of Germany*. New York, Time Life Books, 1969.

Hillman, H. *The Diner's Guide to Wines*. New York, Hawthorn Books Inc., 1978.

Jacobs, J. *Gastronomy*. New York, Newsweek Books, 1975.

Jeffs, J. *Sherry*. London, Faber & Faber, 1982.

Johnson, H. *The World Atlas of Wine*. New York, Simon & Shuster, 1977.

Kroll, R. *The Nahe Region*. German Wine Review, 1982/II.

Maby, P. *A Basic Guide to Cheese*. Toronto, Holt, Linehart & Winton, 1973.

Matuschka-Greiffenclau. *German Wine & Food*. German Wine Review, 1982/II.

Pearl, A.M., Cuttle, C. & Deskins, B. *Completely Cheese*. New York, Middle Village, Jonathan David, 1978.

Pellagrat, H.P. *The Great Book of French Cuisine*. World Publishing Co. 1966.

Peppercorn, D. *Bordeaux*. London, Faber & Faber, 1982.

Petel, P. *The Little Wine Steward*. Toronto, Best Sellers Inc., 1981.

Read, J. *The Wines of Spain*. London, Faber & Faber, 1982.

Robards, T. *The N.Y. Times Book of Wine*. New York, Avon, 1976.

Root, W. *The Food of France*. New York, Random House, 1977.

Root. W. *The Food of Italy*. New York, Random House, 1977.

Schneider, S. *The International Album of Wine*. New York, Vineyard Books, 1977.

Sharp, A. *Winetaster's Secrets*. Toronto, Horizon, 1981.

Sheraton, M. *The German Cookbook*, New York, Random House 1965.

Sichel, P. *The Wines of Germany* (prev. ed. by Frank Schoonmaker). New York, Hastings House, 1982.

Staab, J. *The Rheingau and Its Viticulture*. German Wine Review, 1983/I.

Sutcliffe, S. *The Wine Drinker's Handbook*. London, Marshall Editions, 1982.

Wasserman, S. *The Wines of Italy*. New York, Stein & Day, 1976.

Wine Tidings, Eds. *Gateway to Wine*. Montreal, Kylix International Ltd., 1981.

ABOUT
THE
AUTHOR

Arlene Taveroff is a dietitian, teacher, author, wife, mother and superb cook. She has successfully managed to combine her degree in science and a love of fine food into an exciting and rewarding career.

Arlene's approach to food is both rational and sensory. A slim 5 ft., 5 in., she is living proof that you can combine good nutrition with sensuous pleasure of well prepared food.

Her first experience in wine tasting came as a result of her undergraduate studies in nutrition. As a member of a sensory evaluation team, developing infant formulas for children with metabolic deficiencies, Arlene was required to taste a variety of nutrient components in a variety of combinations. To help motivate the panel, the group leader, one of Arlene's university professors, would occasionally lead the team in a wine tasting, encouraging the students to test their skills on something more enticing than baby food.

As a wine taster, she has never looked back. Now a member of several wine societies, including the Opimian Society, the International Wine and Food Society and the Academie du Vin, Arlene frequently attends tastings, and is constantly examining the effects of different combinations of wine and food. An invitation to the Taveroff home for dinner is a gustatory adventure.